VISION

OTHER BOOKS BY LEONARD E. READ

Romance of Reality
Pattern for Revolt
Instead of Violence
Outlook for Freedom
Goverment: An Ideal Concept
   Governo Um Concito Ideal
Why Not Try Freedom?
   ¿Por Que No Ensayar la Libertad?
Elements of Libertarian Leadership
Anything That's Peaceful
   Todo por la Paz
The Free Market and Its Enemy
   El Enemigo del Mercado Libre
Deeper Than You Think
Accent on the Right
The Coming Aristocracy
Let Freedom Reign
Talking to Myself
Then Truth Will Out
To Free or Freeze
Who's Listening?
Having My Way
Castles in the Air
The Love of Liberty
Comes the Dawn
Awake for Freedom's Sake

LEONARD E. READ

VISION

Foundation for Economic Education
Irvington-on-Hudson, New York 10533

THE AUTHOR AND PUBLISHER

Leonard E. Read (1898–1983) was the founding president of The Foundation for Economic Education.

The Foundation, established in 1946, is a nonpolitical, nonprofit, educational institution. Its senior staff and numerous writers are students as well as teachers of the free-market, private-ownership, limited government rationale. Sample copies of the Foundation's magazine, *The Freeman,* are available on request.

Published March 1978; reprinted

August 2008

ISBN-0-910614-59-8

Copyright Foundation for Economic Education

Printed in U.S.A.

Foundation for Economic Education
30 South Broadway
Irvington-on-Hudson, NY 10533
914.591.7230
www.fee.org

CONTENTS

1. VISION   1

   Where these is no vision—foresight and insight—
   the people perish.

2. LESSONS FROM AFAR   6

   What happened in Argentina has instructions for us.

3. LOOT   11

   A search for words that will more clearly expose
   plunder and shed light on freedom.

4. THE SERVICE MOTIVE   16

   He profits most who serves best!

5. CIVILIZED: RAMROD STRAIGHT   19
   FOR FREEDOM!

   Standing unflinchingly for righteousness distinguishes a civilized man from a barbarian.

6. SOLVING THE ENERGY CRISIS IS SIMPLE   25

   A problem is best solved when everyone is free to try.

7. CHANGES AND EXCHANGES 30

    How free exchange helps us adjust to constant changes.

8. WHY FREEDOM WORKS ITS WONDERS 34

    Tiny bits of expertise on the part of each—when
    free to flow—show forth as the wisdom of the market.

9. THE GUARANTEED LIFE IS A HOAX 39

    The guaranteed life is neither free nor safe.

10. THE FOLLY OF COMPULSION 43

    Compulsion is a disruption of Nature's harmony.

11. WHY NOT SEPARATE SCHOOL
    AND STATE? 48

    Power, when exercised in education or religion,
    tends to corrupt, and absolute power corrupts
    absolutely.

12. ASLEEP AT THE SWITCH 54

    Those who advance civilization and liberty are
    wide awake to their duties and opportunities.

13. QUOTH THE RAVEN, "EVERMORE" 59

    A reversal of Poe's *The Raven*—not sadness, but
    faith and happiness.

14. THIS TIDE OF UNREASON 63

    Passions and emotions direct mob actions; only
    individuals respond to reason.

15. IGNORANCE: AGENT OF DESTRUCTION 67
An assessment of the extent to which the U.S.A.
has adopted the Communist Manifesto.

16. THE SHOW-OFF IS WAY OFF 72

Virtues and talents best show forth when least
flaunted.

17. ON GOING TO EXTREMES 76

Socialism is planned chaos; anarchy is
unplanned chaos.

18. THE ROLE OF SELF-DISCIPLINE 81

Concerning the commensurate exercise of
authority and responsibility.

19. WHY SEEK THE LIGHT? 85

Be not distraught, but for our own and freedom's
sake seek the good.

20. EXPLORE AND EXPLORE AND EXPLORE! 90

The endless road toward revelation is exploration.

21. REFLECTIONS ON PRAISE AND CRITICISM 94

Let praise and criticism be given and received
according to merit.

22. IS THERE TIME ENOUGH? 98

If it is most urgent, there is time enough.

23. WON BY ONE   102

We rise to freedom, not collectively, but by
personal effort and example.

24. OUT OF EVIL: GOOD!   106

Even from the worst of conditions, goodness rises.

25. HUMILITY: THE REMEDY FOR EGOMANIA?   111

Not the power-crazed but only the inquiring
mind is open to Infinite Consciousness.

INDEX   117

TO

The Father of our Country. . . . and to all those who love liberty and are raising a standard to which the wise and honest can repair.

There are two consequences in history: one immediate and instantaneously recognized; the other distant and unperceived at first. These consequences often contradict each other; the former come from our short-run wisdom, the latter from long-run wisdom. The providential event appears after the human event. Behind men rises God. Deny as much as you wish the Supreme Wisdom, do not believe in its action, dispute over words, call what the common man calls Providence "the force of circumstances" or "reason"; but look at the end of an accomplished fact, and you will see that it has always produced the opposite of what was expected when it has not been founded from the first on morality and justice.

—CHATEAUBRIAND
Memoirs from beyond the Tomb

1
VISION

Where there is no vision, the people perish.
—PROVERBS 29:18

Vision is the blessing of foresight, but it has no chance of realization without its companion blessing, *insight*. In the absence of these twin attainments—each within our reach—the people perish; that is, they vegetate rather than germinate, stagnate instead of growing in awareness, perception, consciousness. Vision, therefore—the power of penetrating to reality by mental acuteness—must be developed if our role in human destiny is to be fulfilled.

This commentary is founded, first, on the most remarkable instance of foresight known to me and, second, on an equally remarkable instance of insight. Here is the foresight—by Lord Tennyson (1809–1892), that prescient English poet and poet laureate during the last 42 years of his life:

> For I dipt into the future, far
> as human eye could see,
> Saw the *Vision* of the world and
> all the wonders that would be;
> Saw the heavens fill with commerce,
> argosies of magic sails,
> Pilots of the purple twilight,
> dropping down with costly bales.

1

Saw the heavens fill with commerce, argosies of magic sails—
Tennyson's imagination caught a glimpse of our modern aircraft, the
magic sails being metal wings. "Locksley Hall"—from which the
above lines are quoted—appeared in 1842 when flying machines
were but a dream. Leonardo da Vinci was another of the rare
dreamers; he drew sketches of an airplane four centuries before
Tennyson's time.

Pilots of the purple twilight, dropping down with costly bales—
Air flight, even at night, dropping down with bales—ranging all the
way from bags of fresh spinach, air mail, billions of tons of heavy
freight to millions of individuals—day-in-and-day-out!

Saw the Vision of the world and all the wonders that would be—
Assuredly, Tennyson did not see all the wonders that would be but
what he foresaw startles the imagination. Can his remarkable foresight be explained? It seems unlikely, unless by another blest with
a comparable vision. Who among us in today's world can see that far
into the future with such accuracy and clarity? Who can see the
miracles that will grace Americans in the year 2042? A confession:
I cannot see what's in store for us next year!

There is at least one reason why Tennyson's foresight was
keener than yours, mine, or anyone else's. There have been so many
millions of miracles since his day—each the genesis of countless
others—that scarcely anyone, however gifted, can see today the
wonders in the offing.

To foresee a carriage developing from the wheelbarrow with
which one is familiar is one thing. It is more difficult to foresee in the
wheelbarrow the miracle of that first plane designed and flown by the
Wright brothers. More difficult still—even having seen that first
plane—is to envision in it the miracle of the 747 jet. Every bit of
knowledge gained opens countless new paths into the infinite
unknown—each step forward and upward introducing numerous
variables and complexities as well as opportunities.

Analogous to the above, consider the politico-economic situation
prior to Tennyson's time. Mercantilism—no less authoritarian than
serfdom or feudalism—had hobbled the people. Under that baneful
restraint there were relatively few miracles, and minor ones compared

with those that followed. The potential creativity of countless Englishmen was inhibited. Creativity lay more or less dormant—deadened!

However, about 150 years ago the thoughts and ideas of that great thinker, Adam Smith, were beginning to bear fruit through such spokesmen as John Bright and Richard Cobden. These men understood and clearly explained not only the fallacies of mercantilism but the truth of that absolute principle: freedom in transactions. Tennyson was observing the birth of an enlightenment and foresaw some of its fantastic results.

Doubtless, he reflected on the territory that is now the U.S.A. when the Pilgrims landed at Plymouth Rock. To describe it as underdeveloped would be an understatement. There was no development! Yet, seven generations later, numerous governments sent commissions here to find the secret of our unprecedented prosperity. Their soils were as fertile, climates as friendly and resources as plentiful. Why were most of their citizens in poverty, many starving? What could the answer be?

Tennyson, being deeply observant and having witnessed the wonderful results when the Industrial Revolution replaced mercantilism, must have seen the answer:

- Government limited to keeping the peace and to invoking a common justice;
- The Creator rather than government as the endower of the rights to life and livelihood;
- Fewer man-concocted restraints against the release of creative energy than ever before in all history;
- Inventions, discoveries, insights, intuitive flashes—think-of-thats—by the trillions, and multiplying.

Tennyson's foresight was grounded in politico-economic knowedge.

While making no claim to any such keen foresight, I can foresee not the wonders but the disaster that lies ahead if our present decline into the planned economy and welfare state—socialism—continues. Also, I can foresee a return to the ideal society if that indispensable companion blessing of foresight—insight—becomes more generally known and obeyed.

Edmund Burke gave to posterity an appropriate introduction to the remarkable insight I wish to present: "I hope to see the surest of all reforms, perhaps the only sure reform—the ceasing to do ill." How do we cease to do ill, to be rid of the current socialism? By coming to know—and strictly adhering to—that which is righteous. The Father of our Country, George Washington, bestowed on Americans the insight—the very root of righteousness:

> If to please the people, we offer what we ourselves
> disapprove, how can we afterwards defend our work?
> *Let us raise a standard to which the wise and honest*
> *can repair.* The event is in the hand of God.[1]

There is a correct way to evaluate this wisdom: not using the common tactic of looking upon the errors of others, but rather searching ourselves, the face in the mirror: **ME!**

Do I speak or write to gain favors, wealth, popularity or, if running for office, votes? Or to avoid disagreement or criticism? Is my thinking loaded with "yes, buts" leaks—ways that I know not to be righteous? If so, could I afterwards defend my work? I could not!

How, then do I cease to do ill? By following as nearly as possible Washington's advice: Let us raise a standard to which the wise and honest can repair, in a word, *Exemplarity!* As Burke wrote: "Example is the school of mankind, and they will learn at no other."

In this, my task, my indebtedness is acknowledged—not only to Lord Tennyson and his foresight and to Washington and his insight, but also to Burke who was graced with both foresight and insight. Theirs was an attainment to which I aspire.

"Where there is no vision, the people perish." Where there is vision, the people prosper materially, intellectually, morally, and spiritually. My aim: To acquire Vision!

* * *

---

[1] Attributed to George Washington during the Constitutional Convention.

In this, my 23rd book, there is nothing original except the phrasing, which differs with each of us day by day. As Goethe wrote, "All truly wise ideas have been thought already thousands of times."

The chapters that follow represent one man's striving for vision—foresight and insight; they set forth such findings as I have been able to garner from the wise—past and present. Another source—explained later—is the omnipresent radiation; an "immense intelligence," as Emerson put it. The ability to intercept the beams of this Infinite Wisdom by finite man appears to gain bit by bit as the result of concentration and a prayerful desire for enlightenment. But no one among us, past or present, can claim originality; the origin of wise ideas is far over and beyond the mind of man.

Finally, why do I share these phrasings with others? There are two reasons. First, I wish others to share their thoughts with me. And, second, the more one shares his ideas with others, the more and higher grade are the ideas he receives. Giving or sharing is the precedent to reception. This is an ancient truth to be found in *Acts* XX:35: "It is more blessed to give than to receive."

In the following chapters, I share with you. Now, it is your turn!

2

•—— LESSONS FROM AFAR ——•

*Thy blessings upon our freedom associates—near and far,
past and present—the perfection of our ideas and ideals,
and our strict adherence to them.*

The U.S.A. has been sinking into a socialistic society during the past few decades—with rampant inflation and its consequences. Is it possible for us to learn a lesson from freedom associates in a distant land? I am happy to report that there is a lesson to be learned.

Dr. Benjamin A. Rogge [1920–1980], Professor of Political Economy, Wabash College, and I spent a week in Buenos Aires (June 1977)—the most gratifying seven days I've experienced in my extensive domestic and foreign travels of the past 45 years.

I had first visited Buenos Aires in 1940. Argentina was then one of the world's most productive nations. Its producers adhered more or less to free-market principles and, as a consequence, its people experienced an unusual prosperity. The peso was worth about 33 of our pennies. Keep this in mind: at that time, just 37 years ago, *a 1940 dollar and 3 pesos were of equal value.*

Doubtless, the remarkable prosperity had quite a bit to do with subsequent events. As Horace, the Roman of 2,000 years ago, observed: "Times of adversity have the effect of eliciting talents which in prosperous circumstances would have lain dormant."

In any event, free-market thinking lapsed in the Argentine. Result? A Command Society! As an example, government owned the railroads and the resulting deficits were enormous. But ownership and "operation" of railroads was only one among hundreds of government takeovers. How pay for these inevitable failures? The government merely printed paper money to "make up the difference"—a fantastic dilution of the medium of exchange and an unprecedented inflation.

Argentina was one of the world's major producers and exporters of beef. Could the beef producers sell to the highest bidders? Indeed not! Government compelled each to sell to the government at a far-below-market price and then the government sold to the highest bidders in other nations. These are but samplings of the government's ownership and control, calling to mind our postal system or TVA.

Into this muddle of governmental intervention stepped Perón and the terrorists! Eventually, the nation was freed of this wild dictocrat who escaped to Spain taking millions in gold coin. *But the terrorists remained!* What to do? A military government took over with the aim of restoring sufficient order that peaceful elections might again prevail.

My second visit to Buenos Aires was in April 1958 for a series of lectures under the sponsorship of Centro de Estudios Sobre la Libertad of which the remarkable free-market thinker Alberto Benegas Lynch became president. When I arrived, the military was still in command: General Aramburu, President, and Admiral Rojas, Vice President. I interviewed these men and found them favorably disposed to the freedom philosophy. Shortly after my departure, the military withdrew, feeling all was calm enough to leave the future to a popular election. Frondizi became the new president.

The general and the admiral gave up their rank and retired to private life. However, the terrorists kidnapped the general, took him to their hideout, and later executed this fine man. God bless his soul! The admiral was more fortunate and escaped the maniacs.

However, Frondizi's government was unable to maintain law and order. Finally, the "Peronistas" came back to power through elections in 1973—first with Campora and afterward with Perón when the former resigned. For a couple of years things went from bad to worse. Inflation was rising at the rate of 900 percent annually (more than 75 percent per month). Argentina was in a chaotic situation. Terrorism was getting stronger and stronger. The only possible remedy? Another military government—March 21, 1976—tough and determined to restore order.

Dr. Rogge and I arrived 19 years after I had last been there. What we observed startled our imaginations. The 1977 dollar is worth about one-fourth of the 1940 dollar. Recall that 3 pesos were equal in value to one dollar then. Today, one receives 370 pesos for a 1977 dollar. Meanwhile, in 1969 Argentina had dropped two zeros, converting old pesos to new at 100 to 1. That makes the present peso worth not 1/3rd but roughly 1/50,000th of the 1940 dollar!

In spite of this inflation something fantastic is going on. Samples:

1. Never have we observed better-dressed people.

2. The stores are aglitter with splendid merchandise and excellent service.

3. Rogge and I never tasted better food in this or any other country and at reasonable rates.

4. I bought a pair of the world's best shoes for $43.00— for less than the best shoes in the U.S.A.

True, inflation had gone down from 900 percent to 120 percent. Is this to suggest that all is well in Argentina? Far from it! Many who were wealthy are in poverty. And millions must be suffering from this government-induced inflation. Yet, obviously, there is some kind of miracle at work. If we can find out what it is, we'll have a guideline for our own salvation—a lesson from afar.

The answer has to do with the reason why Dr. Rogge and I were in Buenos Aires. We had not sought this engagement but, rather, the sponsoring organizations invited us: Centro de Estudios Sobre la Libertad and Fundación Bolsa de Comercio. Ever so many in Argentina are searching for help in the restoration and practice of liberty!

Neither of us has ever spent a more intensive week—busy morning, noon, and night with lectures, interviews, luncheons, dinners, the latter often lasting until 11:00 P.M.

The five lectures, beginning at 6:30 P.M. in the stock exchange, had on each occasion from 700 to 800 in attendance. Never had either of us experienced a more enthusiastic response to the freedom philosophy. A question period followed each lecture and the questions were excellent, all in the spirit of inquiry—no confrontations. By 9:00 P.M. we began refreshments and dinner, the number present ranging from 30 to 100, with intensive discussion.

Each day there was a luncheon sponsored by interested groups and organizations. Eating was incidental; we were there primarily to answer questions for a couple of hours.

On Thursday morning of that week, I was asked to address 200 of the Army's officers. I am confident that in general they are in full agreement with the freedom philosophy.

The next morning, Dr. Rogge was invited to address 30 officers of the Navy. Afterward, more than an hour of splendid, brilliant questions.

I delivered the final lecture of our series on Friday evening. Following the question period, there was a standing applause of greater duration than I had ever known—not for me but for the philosophy Dr. Rogge and I had been explaining.

The reason, as I see it, that Argentina's fantastic inflation has not yet destroyed the economy and why productivity is improving, was presented to us some years ago by Thomas Hogshead:

The idea of freedom must grow weak in the hearts of men before it can be killed at the hands of tyrants.

Weak in the hearts of men? Not in Argentina! Never, in all of my experience, have I observed the idea of freedom so strong in the hearts of men as in our recent visit to that country. It is vibrant! Not all the tyrants who ever lived—Perón, Hitler, or the rest—could any more kill this exalted belief than they—in their positions of power—could do away with ignorance. Confronted with an undaunted belief in the freedom way of life, all tyrants become impotent. This belief, and nothing less, will rid humanity of such tyranny—whether of the Argentine or the U.S.A. variety. Up with freedom and away with tyrants!

Success in the form of wealth, fame or whatever—getting ahead of others in any field—is heady stuff. When "What a great man am I!" dominates the mentality, improving talents are not elicited but lie dormant. Argentina's earlier prosperity spawned adversity. This, in turn, elicited the remarkable talents I have just reported.

The same sequence of dormancy and awakening is evident in the United States today. Many individuals in various walks of life are determined to "save free enterprise." This determination is step number one.

It's the second step—unorthodox and thus largely unheeded—that must now be taken. *Ours is not a selling but a learning problem!* Never try to reach for others. Instead, strive for that perfection in understanding and exposition which will cause others to reach for your achievement. Freedom ideas and ideals can never be injected into the consciousness of another; rather, these ideas and ideals must be sought to be absorbed. Rely *exclusively* on the law of attraction.

I am unaware of anyone, in this or any other country, who better understands and can more clearly explain the freedom philosophy than Dr. Rogge. I said "better," not "best." There are others of comparable talent and their number is growing.

Bear in mind that we did not seek the Argentina engagement; they sought us. Is there proof that this unorthodox tactic is correct and effective? Rogge and others of his stature receive more invitations for lectures and interviews than they can possibly accommodate. Emulate these who are striving for personal excellence; then others— if interested in freedom—will seek your tutorship! The free-market, private-ownership, limited-government way of life bears a far higher price than mere yearning. The price tag reads, **LEARNING!**

Finally, a doff of the hat to our Argentine friends: We in *los Estados Unidos* are grateful for your encouragement and enlightenment—lessons from afar!

3

LOOT

He sins as much who holds the sack
as he who fills it. —GABRIEL MEURIER

Richard Weaver wrote a book titled *Ideas Have Consequences*. Ideas do indeed shape our way of life and mold our very being. However, we think in words; and what we mean by the words we use, and what others think we mean by them, may range from the bright lights of creativity to the dark shadows of destruction. The scholarly authors of *The Meaning of Meaning* (Charles Ogden and Ivor Richards) referred to "the tyranny of words," meaning, of course, their misuse and the consequent misunderstanding and confusion. As someone phrased it years ago:

> I know you believe you understand what you think I said. But I am not sure you realize that what you heard is not what I meant.

Not only do we need to know the ideas and practice the ways, we also need the words to explain how freedom works its wonders. And what words will best describe and explain freedom's opposite? How does one make it clear that accepting coercively confiscated "benefits" is just as sinful as the confiscation itself? It would seem self-evident that if no one would accept Social Security payments there would be no governmental plundering to finance the program. And the same is true of thousands of other ignoble schemes.

"He sins as much who holds the sack as he who fills it." The acceptance of plunder is as sinful as the plundering itself. But where are the words to portray the sinful nature of plunder?

Many of us, over the years, have used the words "special privilege" to describe freedom's opposite—the plundering way of life. But these words no longer serve to describe the undesirable; they have lost their derogatory impact. So widespread is the practice of plunder that what were at one time devised as special grants of political power—and were more or less clearly recognized as such—are now claimed as the inalienable rights of the special class spawned by such privileges. Among pigs at the trough, there is no stigma attached to the specialist; he may indeed be considered more saint than sinner.

So, why not use another word that has a chance of clarifying our meaning? Let's try an acronym—the first letters of several truly definitive words: Living Off Others Thoughtlessly—LOOT!

Looting is an accurate synonym for plundering and still carries a sharp verbal sting which most of us would rather avoid. Nevertheless, many among us today are *thoughtlessly* living off the labor of others.

Throughout history there have been looters of this or that variety. But we seem now to be confronted with a *progression* of such harmful behavior. As more and more people have abandoned moral scruples—feathering their nests at the expense of others—looting in its countless forms has more and more become a way of life.

Emerson wrote, "Thought is the seed of action." Honest, moral, and sound economic thought results in commendable and creative action; each person serves himself through serving others. But if dishonest, immoral, and uneconomic thinking prevails, the results must be harmful, not only to others but to self as well. Such thoughtlessness, then—rather than careful thought—is the seed of actions which presently bedevil us. And the seeds, more often than not, are words with garbled meanings, such as the twisted meaning of "special privilege"—warped from bad to good. The tyranny of words!

It is increasingly evident that countless millions in all walks of life thoughtlessly "live" off others; they loot and they don't know it. They are the unwitting victims of their own naïveté, stumbling along the devolutionary road.

Does a professional thief think of himself as a looter? No, he probably thinks of himself as a professional. He has only a primitive or stunted mentality, like the tribesmen of yore who raided distant tribes and made off with what they thoughtlessly regarded as theirs. Economically illiterate—but innocent!

So, we have in the professional crook an unconscious looter suffering no mental pains but glorying in his "gains." Exceptional? No, tens of millions fall into this identical category, and with pride instead of guilt.

Frederic Bastiat helps us to see through this shameful practice:

See if the law [government] takes from some persons what belongs to them, and gives it to other persons to whom it does not belong. See if the law benefits one citizen at the expense of another *by doing what the citizen himself cannot do without committing a crime*.[1]

It is obvious that government would not take from some and give to others were the others to reject the loot. It follows then, that the recipients of ill-gotten gains are as sinful as the government which effects the transfer by force.

Only the hardened professional criminals—a fraction of the population—would personally so indulge themselves. The vast majority would refrain from immoral action were it a you-and-me relationship. Honesty would prevail.

However, when government does the coercive taking and handing out, most citizens—those who do no thinking for themselves—are relieved of any sense of indulging in crimes. Instead they experience a false sense of absolution. Their lack of vision obscures reality!

In compiling a list of looters, let us take care not to confine it just to the "beneficiaries" of food stamps, Medicare, rent control, federal housing projects, workers paid not to work or farmers not to farm, and countless thousands of others engaged in more or less obvious forms of looting. In fairness, we must label all looting as such, and much of it is far from obvious. We must include all instances where

----

[1] From *The Law* by Frederic Bastiat (Irvington-on-Hudson, N.Y.: Foundation for Economic Education).

coercion, be it private or public, is employed to "benefit" some at the expense of others. The list is too long to count, let alone explain, so a few samplings must suffice.

- In St. Louis it was a Gateway Arch that taxpayers from every state were compelled to help finance. Elsewhere, a school, library, park, dam, housing project, or whatever. Is there a community in the U.S.A. without one or more such monuments to looting?

- Minimum-wage laws coercively invoked, with strong support from labor unions, cause large-scale unemployment, the burdens of which all taxpayers are compelled to share. This, too, is a form of looting.

- Strikers by the thousands quit their jobs, and the law makes it impossible for others to accept the jobs the strikers have vacated. More unemployment, less productivity, higher prices and taxes—consumers and taxpayers looted!

- Businessmen and their associations obtain legal prohibitions of free exchange, such as tariffs, embargoes, and quotas. They are no less looters than are the striking workmen. How is this looting done? All others are deprived of the opportunity to produce in those fields—the looting or limitation of their livelihood and their lives.

At this point, let us be mindful of that old adage, "the pot calling the kettle black." For we critics of looting may be looters ourselves. Plundering is so rampant that everyone is involved more or less—unconsciously participating or trapped beyond escape. Doubtless, you are trapped in the Social Security "lootery." I am trapped in the socialistic mail "system." Examples abound. This predicament poses the final question: What should we critics of looting do? What might the right tactic be?

Perhaps another acronym may help to clarify the creative force: Living In Good High Thought: **LIGHT**!

To see the **LIGHT** we need what I would call intellectual binoculars. We should see, not with just one, but with both eyes.

The vast majority see with one eye only and, as a consequence, observe merely surface or false appearances. Being half-blind results in discouragement and frustration; it lacks any creative stimulus— life's mission abandoned.

Fortunately, there are those who see with one eye the falseness of **LOOT**, and with the other observe the true **LIGHT**. To thus see beneath the surface brings enlightenment—encouragement. Such persons are aware of the growing numbers who are beginning to see the destructiveness of plunder and how freedom works its unbelievable wonders.

The half-blind see only the shadows. Those with "intellectual binoculars" can share the insight of Goethe:

> Where the light is brightest,
> the shadows are darkest.

4
─── THE SERVICE MOTIVE ───

*Think success, and you will automatically
create the circumstances and the movements leading to success.*
—MICHAEL LOMBARDI

As Ralph Waldo Emerson wrote, "An institution is the lengthened shadow of one man." The one man, an outstanding exemplar and practitioner of this thesis, was a Japanese—Konosuke Matsushita.[1] Born with a silver spoon in his mouth? Quite the opposite:

> Yet all he had to start with in life were "three disadvantages": he was in dire poverty; he was forced to quit school to work as an errand boy at the age of nine; and he was so frail in health that several times he resigned himself to imminent death.

Did he overcome his disadvantages? He developed the largest and most profitable business in Japan's history!

Instead of being born with a silver spoon in his mouth, he was born with a golden idea in his head. Here it is:

●───────

[1] See *The Matsushita Phenomenon* by Rowland Gould (Tokyo: The Diamond Publishing Co., Ltd., 1970).

He began by thinking about abundance and decided that *the mission* of a manufacturer should be to take scarce resources, convert them into products, making them available at decreasing prices that a better life might be had by all!

Reflect on such an unusual—indeed, exceptional—mission by a manufacturer. While Matsushita insisted on profitability as the true measure of management efficiency, he explicitly forbade the pursuit of profit as the motivation of his business. The motivation must be better and better products at lower and lower prices. He cast his eye on service—serving the consumer[2]—rather than profitability. By so doing, his customers had more for less and a remarkable profitability was the result: the true measure of management efficiency.

Materially, this man began in abject poverty; physically, he was frail; intellectually, he was graced with a wholesome motivation and the good thoughts that made it workable. For him, good thoughts were the wellspring of material success and a life of creative activity. Let us hope that good thoughts may direct our lives as well!

Am I suggesting that the great thought—the service motive—was original with Matsushita? No, but he may have thought it was. Countless persons have had this thought; it popped into their heads, as we say. Wrote Goethe: "All truly wise thoughts have been thought already thousands of times."

This truly wise thought was phrased in resplendent clarity by Arthur F. Sheldon *previous* to its adoption and practice by Matsushita:

The science of business is the science of service and he profits most who serves best.

Sheldon's statement was adopted as the motto of Rotary International—members by the hundreds of thousands in this and other countries.

There is no way of telling how many Rotarians are inspired by and heed their adopted motto, or merely give it lip service. Perhaps, as with ever so many others in today's U.S.A., the service motto is

---

[2] For an excellent article relating to Matsushita's motivation see "Caveat Emptor: The Consumer's Badge of Authority" by Professor Bertel Sparks (*The Freeman*, June 1975).

practiced with no reference to or awareness of wise admonitions. When men are free to try, countless thousands are motivated by an ever-improving service to consumers. To those with good minds, *casting the eye aright comes naturally!*

The success of service! I have friends who are in business all by themselves whose sole motivation is service. They think success, practice the key to success, and automatically create the circumstances and movements leading to success.

Further, I am acquainted with managements of small and large corporations who not only have service as their motivation but instill this same high objective in their associates. The result is the same as in Matsushita's case: employees work not *for* but *with* these managements. A teamwork glorious to behold! When and if service is the root, the flower is profit. *He profits most who serves best!*

All of us should remember and repeat this great truth by Edmund Burke: "Example is the school of mankind; they learn at no other." Many thousands of businessmen—small and large operations—are lamenting the very low esteem in which business is held by the public. And, mostly, they are resorting to all sorts of schemes to restore respect and confidence in business. Many of these schemes are doing more harm than good. The only remedy? Exemplary conduct! The millions in the school of mankind will learn only by *example*.

Let service be the motive, that Golden Idea in the head of entrepreneurs. Such exemplarity will curb the tendency to defame the producers of goods and services. There'll be a turnabout: the beneficiaries will pay homage to those who serve them best.

If those of us in business will adhere to the service motive, then the right—freedom to act creatively as anyone chooses—will prevail.

5
CIVILIZED: RAMROD STRAIGHT FOR FREEDOM!

To realize the relative validity of one's convictions and yet stand for them unflinchingly is what distinguishes a civilized man from a barbarian.[1]
—JOSEPH A. SCHUMPETER

Having spent several hours with this remarkable economist at his home in 1946 following his retirement from Harvard, I know what he meant by "one's convictions." He embraced freedom in precisely the same sense as we at FEE mean it—freedom to act creatively as anyone pleases. This is what Schumpeter stood for, and in my view he ranks among the top economists of all time. What a thinker and scholar!

On one point, however, I disagree with him. He contended that our ideal way of life had gone so far down the drain that there was no hope of recovery. His assessment of the future was pessimistic. Mine is the opposite. I have faith that *we are going to win!* True, winning will be a miracle but I believe with Goethe that "Miracle is the darling child of *Faith*."

---

[1] *Capitalism, Socialism and Democracy* (New York: Harper Bros., 1950 [1942]).

The barbarian is defined as "a man in a rude uncivilized state." Barbarism is composed of specific acts. Only rarely in our time is there anyone whose every action is barbaric—in the common use of that term. The lowest form of barbarism is practiced by those who feast on their fellows—cannibals. For all we know, there may be a few among such tribes who refuse to so indulge—a step away from such inhumanity.

However, let not the citizens of today's U.S.A. bask unduly in their civility. Reflect on the many millions who feast, not on human flesh, but on life-sustaining goods and services—private property—taken coercively from others. Feasting on others has, to our disgrace, become a way of life. Is this any less barbaric than cannibalism? Only less apparent, that's all. Feasting on others without their consent, here or wherever, is not civilized!

What does it mean to be civilized? It means "to give order, law and culture to; humanize, reclaim from savagery; to transfer from military to civil jurisdiction."

To give order, law and culture to—culture, as defined by Matthew Arnold—"acquainting ourselves with the best that has been known and said in the world"—can grace only the exceptional few, unless there be law and order. Those of us devoted to the good society—the freedom way of life—cherish everyone's freedom to grow, emerge, evolve. The extent to which others are growing in awareness, perception, consciousness dramatically enlarges your and my cultural opportunities.

It should be obvious that there can be no order without law. In a "civilization" featured by cave dwellers, cannibals, vigilantes, or anarchists, all is helter-skelter—confusion reigns! The good society requires legal restrictions against destructive actions, which leaves all citizens free to act creatively as they please. The law, in an ideal society, is strictly limited to keeping the peace and invoking a common justice. The free and unfettered market reigns, with its remarkable wisdom, and culture blooms!

Humanize, reclaim from savagery—The definition of humanize is "to make human; give a human nature or character to. To make humane; make kind, merciful, considerate; *civilize*, refine." Thus does mankind emerge from savagery.

When the primitive, barbaric notion of government—*"to exercise authority over; direct; control; rule; manage"*—prevails as it now does, our "civilization" is in a state of savagery. Political cannibals—little know-it-alls—control our lives!

The ascent from savagery reached its apogee in the U.S.A. when the Constitution and the Bill of Rights limited government more than ever before. Result? Law and order![2]

In that glorious step toward the ideal society responsibility for self replaced political barbarism. Not only did self-responsibility engender self-reliance but it inspired humans to become humane. Such virtues as kindness, mercy, charity, and consideration for others became a way of life. Civilized!

It is an observed fact that when government pre-empts any activity, be it welfare or whatever, nearly everyone gives up all thought as to how he or she would behave were self-responsibility the mode. If a neighbor is starving, they shrug their shoulders—"That's the government's chore." What if there were no political barbarism? These very persons would share their last loaf of bread! However, in the absence of savagery—when freedom reigns—there would be no starving neighbors!

To transfer from military to civil jurisdiction—Until 1776 men had been killing each other by the millions over the age-old question as to which form of authoritarianism—military jurisdiction—should preside as sovereign. The argument had not been military versus civil jurisdiction, but only between this or that military form. And then, in 1776, the greatest wisdom ever written into a political document:

> . . . that all men are . . . endowed by their Creator with certain unalienable Rights, that among these are Life, Liberty, and the pursuit of Happiness.

By unseating government as sovereign—resting sovereignty in the individual as endowed by the Creator—the new nation experienced a transfer from military to civil jurisdiction. This act, and this alone,

---

[2] See "Eruptions of Truth" in my book *Awake for Freedom's Sake* (Irvington, N.Y.: Foundation for Economic Education).

explains the American miracle—the greatest outburst of creative energy ever known—truly a *civilized act!*

But if that action was an upward step toward a civilized U.S.A., what shall be said of recent developments? Military jurisdiction again, that is, countless edicts—Federal, state, and local—backed by armed force: barbarism! How are we to reverse this latest trend? Let us reflect on Schumpeter's way of drawing the distinction between a civilized man and a barbarian, for the remedy is exclusively in the hands of civilized men.

"To realize the relative validity of one's convictions," in Schumpeter's case, meant a personal commitment to the validity of private ownership, the free and unfettered market and government strictly limited to keeping the peace and invoking a common justice. He was ramrod straight!

It is the absence of such convictions, as exhibited by people in every walk of life, that presently plagues "the land of the free and the home of the brave." By and large, the freedom way of life has few champions and a small following. Finding a Schumpeter among economists is as difficult as finding a statesman among officeholders!

Who are the beneficiaries of successful enterprises—those businesses, large and small, that supply goods and services? We, the consumers, all of us! Were enlightened self-interest to prevail, the benefactors—the suppliers—no less than the beneficiaries would stand ramrod straight for freedom. The distressing fact? Most individuals in either capacity are befuddled—confusion reigns! What, pray tell, can the remedy be?

In what occupational category might we expect the largest percentage of individuals standing foursquare for such ideas as private ownership, the freedom to exchange, the right to cooperate or compete, plus all the other virtues related to entrepreneurship? Would it not be among entrepreneurs themselves—businessmen? Yet, it is almost in vain that one searches there for a champion or exemplar.

Why? Perhaps no one knows all the answers. It may be that the competitive struggle so distracts them that they give little serious thought to the principles underlying the market economy. This is regrettable, for we know that good practice stems exclusively from good ideas, that is, freedom ideas.

There is only one remedy: the ascendancy of good ideas. As Arthur Shenfield wrote:

> *If the businessman does not learn to understand the importance of ideas, he will find himself the slave of the ideas of his enemies.* But on the other hand he is fatally ready to accommodate himself to his enemies' ideas, and even to finance their propagation, if they are presented with an attractive varnish. . . . And see how readily he swallows the fraudulent concept of the "social responsibility of business," which is one of his enemies' best weapons for breaking down his defenses. See also how he will make munificent gifts to universities and foundations whose faculties or staffs are busily engaged in undermining the free enterprise system.[3]

The remedy—good ideas—however, applies not only to businessmen but to all of us. So let us hear and heed Schumpeter's way for distinguishing a civilized from a barbaric person.

Those who earnestly espouse the freedom way of life are a tiny fraction of our present population, and even among these many do more to harm our cause than to help it! In what manner? Lacking the understanding and courage to proclaim and stand for their convictions, they "leak," that is, they bend to popular opinion which currently rejects freedom.

As Ovid wrote, "We are tardy in believing when belief brings hurt." What hurts these weaklings? It is disapproval, neighborhood or social ostracism, being frowned upon, unpopularity, avoidance, and the like. "Silence is golden, sometimes *yellow*." How golden it would be if such persons remained silent, for in their half-hearted efforts they do more harm to freedom than those who openly support the command society.

Schumpeter's *standing unflinchingly*—ramrod straight for freedom—is what distinguishes a civilized man from a barbarian. Is "the welfare state" way of feasting off others any less barbarous than direct cannibalism?

───────

[3] See "Lessons from the British Experience" by Arthur Shenfield (*Imprimis*, Vol. 6, No. 4), Hillsdale College, Hillsdale, Michigan.

To stand unflinchingly for what one believes is *integrity*: the accurate reflection in word and deed of what one believes to be righteous. Indeed, cannibalism would quickly disappear were the opponents of freedom to reflect in word and deed the nonsense they presently espouse. Even they would find the process revolting.

Intellectual honesty is the formula for a return to freedom in society, precisely because it is the formula for individual growth and achievement. It is far more joyous to seek praise from God—righteousness—than from men. So, let us side not only with Joseph Schumpeter but with the Father of our Country, George Washington:

I hope I shall always possess firmness and virtue enough to maintain what I consider the most enviable of all titles, *the character of an honest man.*

6
SOLVING THE ENERGY CRISIS IS SIMPLE

The Delphic oracle said I was the wisest of all the Greeks. It is because that I alone of all the Greeks, know that I know nothing. —SOCRATES

The U.S.A. is faced with an energy crisis—no doubt about it. Countless thousands of bureaucrats, involved businessmen, "economists," and others are advancing so-called solutions they "think" are right—no doubt about that! Except that nearly everyone overlooks the simple and only solution; otherwise, they all differ—no two alike.

Why are we in an energy crisis? It's because the "solutions" are founded on a false assumption, namely, "I know the answer." For the truth, hear Thomas Alva Edison: "No one knows more than a millionth of one per cent of anything." It's these egotistical assumptions that brought on the crisis, and it's these very same assumptions that will worsen rather than better the mess we're in unless the simple remedy gains understanding.

The simple remedy? Both Socrates and Edison gave us the answer which, if followed, would read like this: "It is because I, among millions of Americans, am one who knows nothing and knows it." It is necessary, however, that neither you nor I should be *alone* in this wise confession. Let there be a reasonable number of us and then,

25

lo and behold, the miracle—the rescue—by that fantastic wisdom which exists *alone* in the free and unfettered market.

With the above as an introduction, let's have a glance at the enormity of energy. No more than a glance is possible for no one ever has or ever will assess it in totality. For instance, the energy we earthlings enjoy is generally assumed to have its origin in our star. According to my dictionary the sun is:

> . . . the incandescent body of gases about which the earth and other planets revolve and which furnishes light, heat, and energy for the solar system.

Here is another assumption which, until now, I had not questioned:

Although less than half of the earth's sunlight entering the earth's atmosphere reaches its surface, just 40 minutes of that solar input equals all the energy mankind consumes in an entire year.

Three questions pop into mind:

1. Isn't it possible that there is something in Creation that precedes the sun as source? We don't know one millionth of one percent of anything, let alone this.

2. Are there not untold forms of energy beyond the range of solar energy?

3. Why has there not been a greater use of solar energy in the light of present energy shortages?

As a sampling of the thousand and one kinds of energy, reflect on electrical energy. There is not a person who is even aware of its many uses. They range from tiny services like electric toothbrushes and electric razors to such enormous outpourings of kilowatt-hours as in metal melting—steel, aluminum, and the like.

----

[1] See "Tapping the Sun's Energy" by David G. Lee (*National Wildlife*, August–September 1974).

Until 1864 the human voice could be transmitted the distance a shouter could be heard—about the length of a football field—at the speed that sound can travel. Now? Around the world in that same fraction of a second—at the speed of light. The phenomenon of electrical energy!

To repeat, electrical energy has a thousand and one uses and not a living person understands a single one of them. Why this bald assertion? *No one knows what electricity is!* Thus, where is the person who can solve our increasing electrical shortages? Wiseacres galore, but not one remotely wise enough! This should be self-evident.

The above is no more than a glance at the energy problem. Suppose someone were to write a book on all the forms he could bring to mind: Energy stored in such known fuels as gas, oil, coal, wood; magnetic energy, solar energy, gravitational forces, wind, waterpower; heat, light, sound, electrical and chemical energy; nuclear energy, tension, motion, friction; animal power, human energy. Still, no more than a glance!

Countless kinds of energy supplement human energy. And note how variable the latter—from all sorts of physical exertions to such mental efforts as thinking and writing. No two persons are identical in this respect; indeed, each of us varies from day to day.

The only point I am attempting to emphasize is that no one has the slightest idea how, by himself, to solve the energy crisis, egotistical pretensions to the contrary notwithstanding! Am I contending that the problem has no solution? No, the solution is so simple that nearly everyone ignores it.

Here are several thoughts that pave the way to the simple answer. Even though no one knows what electricity is, countless individuals with their tiny bits of expertise—when freely flowing—have discovered how to harness it. Likewise, no one really knows what solar energy is but the means of harnessing it have been discovered and employed in a few minor instances. Why not on a larger scale? Because the government has intervened to the point that private effort is discouraged, leaving the wisdom of the market dormant.

To illustrate: Some years ago we had a water shortage along the Hudson River. Car washing, lawn sprinkling, and the like were forbidden. Restaurants, short of special requests, were not allowed to serve a glass of water. Why that economic crisis? Government pre-empted—socialism—instead of the free market where the wisdom is.

Even more striking was an experience some months ago on the Monterey Peninsula. In every bathroom were printed instructions: flush toilets only when absolutely necessary, confine showers to one minute, and so on. There we were on the shore of the world's largest body of water: the Pacific Ocean. A water shortage! And for precisely the same reason as our water shortage on the Hudson.

The art of desalinization has been known for several decades. However, the process lies largely dormant due to a preponderance of those who say, "I know the answer." They have convinced themselves and the masses that no other solutions than their own would be worth trying—blind leaders of the blind.

I am confident that if the market were trusted to operate, water would be abundantly available, not only along the Pacific Coast but miles inland as well, at a surprising low price. The wisdom of the market is far greater and more productive than can be mustered through planned coercion.

How explain the simple solution to the energy crisis? It's as simple as two times two is four.

In 1958 I wrote an article entitled "I, Pencil." This explained that no person knows how to make such a simple thing as an ordinary wooden lead pencil. The article has since been distributed and read throughout the United States and other countries, without a single contradiction in all these years. In 1958 there were produced in our country *1,600,000,000* wooden lead pencils, despite the fact that not a person on earth had the combination of knowledge and skill to make one!

It may be true that no one knows more than one millionth of one percent of anything. But a pencil consists of many millions of *somethings*—tiny bits of expertise—flowing and configuring. The free and unfettered market has indeed a wisdom trillions of times greater than the wisdom of one who claims, "I know the answer."

The making of a pencil is a simple operation compared to the desalinization of water or to any of the major phases of our so-called energy problems. So, leave the solutions to the market where the wisdom is.

Socrates' secret was the knowledge that he didn't know everything. Therefore, let us recognize with him the vital possibility that everyone knows a fraction of this or that. However tiny one's portion may be, let it be freely productive, for in freedom do we best serve ourselves and others.

7
CHANGES AND EXCHANGES

Weep not that the world changes—
did it keep a stable, changeless state
'twere cause indeed to weep.
—WILLIAM CULLEN BRYANT

Though a lawyer and long-time editor, William Cullen Bryant (1794–1878) was most famous as a poet of nature. The paper which he edited and partly owned—the New York *Evening Post*—was renowned for its literary correctness and was a leading free-trade, antislavery journal.

Here we have a top-ranking freedom devotee who had an unusual grasp of nature—Creation—and could put the truths he grasped into enlightening verse, as the above testifies.

Not only is the universe in constant change but so is each of us. Most of us, however, strive for "a stable, changeless state"— an affront to natural law.

Changes in the universe are of a variety and velocity beyond our comprehension. Our galaxy is but one of a seemingly infinite number of galaxies in an expanding universe; it has some 30 billion stars, each of which is in constant, enormous change. That cloud in the sky never had another like it in the world's history, nor is it the same as it was a second ago. No two atoms or snowflakes or blades of grass have ever been the same. The entire universe is a moving, changing phenomenon.

There's a tiny planet in that universe, and one of the inhabitants of the tiny planet—man—is a moving, changing phenomenon, as is all else in nature. We humans, as do the clouds or suns or galaxies, differ from moment to moment. Difficult to imagine is the fact that a quintillion (1,000,000,000,000,000,000) atoms exchange in each individual *every second*! From whence and to where in the universe no one knows or ever will. We should grasp the profound meaning of this if we are to prosper materially, intellectually, morally, and spiritually. Several sages share Bryant's understanding:

> Look abroad thro' Nature's range,
> Nature's mighty law is change.
>
> *—Burns*

> All things are changed, and with them we, too, Change.
> Now this way and now that turns fortune's Wheel.
>
> *—Lotharius I*

> All things must change
> To something new, to something strange.   *—Longfellow*

> There's nothing constant in the universe,
> All ebb and flow, and every shape that's born
> Bears in its womb the seeds of change.   *—Ovid*

> There is nothing permanent except change.   *—Heraclitus*

> In the course of time, we grow to love things we once hated
> and hate things we loved.   *—Stevenson*

Over the years I have known numerous individuals who once loved communism and changed to the point of hating that ignoble creed. Later? Some of them loved liberty! Also, over the past 60 years, I have observed countless citizens—from all walks of life—who once claimed to love liberty whose love changed to hate. Now? They love the planned economy and the welfare state. In what respect does this welfarism differ "from each according to his ability, to each according to his need"—communism? Not one whit!

As related to slavery and freedom, Robert Louis Stevenson's statement is valid; love and hate are appropriate. And in ever so many relationships his sentence could be rephrased to read: In the course of time, we grow to like things we once disliked and to dislike things formerly liked. Reflect on the *things* liked and now disliked. Or, on the *persons* who have switched allegiance. "Nature's mighty law is change," indeed!

In their blindness to reality, many present-day Americans strive for "a stable, changeless state"—an affront to nature's law. And this accounts in no small measure for the U.S.A.'s plunge into socialism— "cause indeed to weep." So, let us try to explain that changes and exchanges are two inseparable parts of nature's law at the human level. It is the change that gives rise to the need for exchange; and the former without the latter has to spell disaster.

Our countrymen by the millions, particularly our elected and appointed political representatives—federal, state, and local— unaware of our ever-changing nature, are determined to stabilize existing conditions, maintain a status quo!

What a coincidence! While on a flight to St. Louis, and just after writing the above paragraph, I overheard a spirited conversation across the aisle and caught this remark: "Ram it down their necks!" Who are some of these "rammers"? They are the stabilizers, those who would coercively cast us in their images. Briefly, they would freeze us at their own level. They are the unwitting enemies of human evolution.

Implicit in evolving is transformation to ever higher levels. The evolution of mankind does not stem from individuals stagnated at this or that level—from a stable, changeless state—but from a growth in awareness, perception, consciousness. Were it not for growth—changing mankind would still be at the Cro-Magnon level. But the know-it-alls are blind to this fact of human nature.

Wrote Sir William Hamilton: "The highest *reach* of human science is the scientific *recognition* of human ignorance."

Reach, indeed! No one can move away from ignorance and toward intelligence who is not forever reaching, striving for enlightenment. One does not *grow* old or ignorant. One becomes old and ignorant by not growing!

Recognition? What is it we must grasp? Not only how infinitesimal is our know-how and the enormity of our ignorance, but how vastly each of us differs from all others! And, this above all: *The ever-changing self!*

When any individual gains an awareness of nature's law, he will never approve of "a stable, changeless state." Such would be comparable to making human tombstones of ourselves—a deadened humanity.

What does the good life require? Free and unfettered exchanges, bearing in mind the tiny, varying bits of expertise which must constantly flow if we are to prosper materially and intellectually. Is it not self-evident that I cannot live on my ever-changing "bits," nor you on yours?

The issue is, shall we freeze or free? Having no faith in human tombstones, and believing in freedom of choice and free exchanges of *all* creative actions, I choose freedom.

Let us fervently pray that a few others may so choose:

LET FREEDOM REIGN!

8
WHY FREEDOM WORKS ITS WONDERS

Here is my explanation of why men, when free to try and to act creatively as they please, produce miracles by the millions. Is mine the right and final answer? No such claim is warranted by me on this subject or by anyone on any subject. Nevertheless, I am bound to seek for and to share with others that which seems to be right.

The wise man referred to by the English dramatist Congreve (1670–1729) was Socrates. It wasn't that this great Greek knew nothing. Everyone above the moronic level knows a wee bit of something. The wisdom of Socrates might be thus paraphrased:

The more I know the more I know there is to know.
The more I see the more I know there is to be seen.

Not many of us see ourselves in this light. Only rarely do we encounter anyone who is keenly aware that the more he knows the more he knows he doesn't know. Yet, in this Socratic wisdom lies the explanation as to why freedom works its wonders.

Interestingly, freedom serves us well despite our unawareness. Why, then, dwell on the matter? The danger is that those who haven't the slightest idea of how little they know will become our masters. Indeed, we have, for some time, been on that deplorable road. The know-it-alls have been gaining and exercising political power. So, it's high time that power be withdrawn. How? Socratic wisdom is the key.

How explain that the more I know the more I know there is to know or the more I see the more I know there is to be seen? The answer relates to the distinction between Infinite Consciousness—the limitless unknown—and finite consciousness—our infinitesimal bits of know-how.

To assist in making the point here at issue, visualize a blackboard having no boundaries—none whatsoever—the unknown. Next, with white chalk draw a circle the size of a silver dollar to symbolize consciousness achieved, say, ten years ago. Now, draw a circle five feet in diameter to symbolize today's consciousness—an admirable growth. But take note of this fact: the circumference, the exposure to darkness—the unknown—is nearly 100 times that of a decade ago! *The more a growth in consciousness is experienced, the nearer one comes to a realization that he knows nothing.* Socrates was wise, indeed!

Unfortunately, those who experience no growth in awareness, perception, consciousness won't understand my illustration either. Unless one is daily becoming more and more aware of how little he knows or sees, he is not growing! Rather, he is dying on the vine, as the saying goes—stalemated! Thank heaven there are individuals who experience growth and who can see why freedom works its wonders—admittedly, an elusive truth.

We need only keep these points in mind:

1. A realization that every individual, regardless of pompous claims to the contrary, knows next to nothing.

2. Among the more than 200 million persons who inhabit the U.S.A., no two are remotely alike. Each possesses, at best, a wee bit of expertise unlike that of any other individual.

3. The only wisdom that graces us with an abundance of goods and services stems *exclusively* from these millions of

infinitesimal know-hows freely flowing and configurating. Every one of these blessings is an aggregation of tiny think-of-thats—no exceptions!

To me, it is self-evident that we should leave all creative activities—education or whatever—to the free and unfettered market where the wisdom is. What can be more absurd than leaving our welfare to those who have no awareness that they know not, that is, to such low-grade ignorance.

No one knows how to make such a simple thing as an ordinary wooden lead pencil. So, what about complex things such as a 747 jet airplane? That transportation marvel has about 4,500,000 parts, and not a man on earth knows how to make any one of these parts. When aloft in one of these miracles of the market, I often reflect on a remarkable blessing: the Socratic wisdom.

As I have written before, "What gives socialism the *appearance* of working is the freedom socialism has not yet destroyed."[1] Or phrase it this way: What gives those who are unaware of their know-nothing-ness the *appearance* of being responsible for our prosperity is the wisdom of the market they have not yet eliminated.

Appearances! How false and misleading most of them are, particularly in the politico-economic realm. Here are several thoughts on appearances by a few graced with Socratic wisdom, including Socrates himself:

Judge not according to the appearance.   *—John 7:24*

Always scorn appearance, and you always may.   *—Emerson*

We should look to the mind, and not to the outward appearance.
—Aesop

We are deceived by the appearance of right.   *—Horace*

There is no trusting in appearance.   *—Sheridan*

---

[1] See "American Mirage" in my book *Awake for Freedom's Sake.*

Don't rely too much on labels
For often they are fables. —*Spurgeon*

You look wise. Pray correct that error. —*Lamb*

The final good and the supreme duty of the wise man
is to resist appearance. —*Cicero*

Beware, so long as you live, of judging men by their outward
appearance. —*La Fontaine*

The shortest and surest way to live with honor in the world,
is to be in reality what we would appear to be. —*Socrates*

As to how we should proceed not only to preserve but to increase
the wonders wrought by freedom, the answer is as easy to state as it
is difficult to accomplish.

Pay no heed to appearances! Look clearly through the political fog!

In appraising a person, whether he be in or out of office, examine
his avowed principles. Should the individual claim a devotion to
freedom, then determine if his practices are consistent therewith—
no "buts," no "leaks"! If his practices belie his preaching, place no
faith in him. But if he consistently practices the freedom he espouses,
he will be a worthy partner in explaining where the wisdom is and
why its miraculous accomplishments.

For encouragement, reflect on the growing number who are
coming to light as partners in this intellectual enterprise. We discover
more and more of them from the near and ancient past. And I am
personally acquainted with several thousand who have achieved this
goal in recent years. But even more encouraging are the countless
thousands seeking and discovering this truth, not a fraction of one
percent of whom ever heard of you or me or we of them. The point
is that any friend of freedom is a friend of yours and mine. None of
us stands alone.

To claim that the wisdom in the free and unfettered market is a
trillion times greater than possessed by any single person would be a

gross understatement. Of one point we can be certain: there are enough individuals sufficiently wise to see through all the sham and to capture and exemplify this truth.

THE TRUTH SHALL MAKE YOU FREE!

9
THE GUARANTEED LIFE IS A HOAX

The guaranteed life turns out to be not only not free—it's not safe.

—MAXWELL ANDERSON

A way of life neither free nor safe is to be shunned; a way of life, as free and safe as reality permits, is to be sought!

Few there are who will disagree with these obvious truisms as to what should be shunned and what sought. Agreement with the obvious is within nearly everyone's range, yet only one in thousands is aware of the fakery implicit in the promises of a guaranteed life— a political hoax rapidly on the increase. And the citizens who are making helpful contributions to a reversal—or even thinking about it—are still fewer in number. Indeed, most people in all walks of life are quite unconsciously working not only against their own but against everyone's self-interest. So, Maxwell Anderson's theme of several decades ago would seem to warrant some renewed observations.

Perhaps the "guaranteed life" here at issue can best be introduced by a brief commentary on the promises men do and do not—can and cannot—live by.

Whether or not a promise is constructive or destructive depends on what is promised. Those who promise to pay their debts, keep their contracts, and exchange their goods and services as represented—assuming fulfillment—are constructive. In the absence of such honesty, life would be diminished and reduced to misery—if indeed it could continue at all.

What I call destructive promises are those that cannot and should not be kept. They make certain, if continued on a large scale, that life will be diminished and miserable. Who are those who make such promises? They are the millions, in and out of office, who propose ideas impossible of fulfillment. These lie at the root of the guaranteed life, a way of life that is not only not free—it is not safe!

There is no way to explain the extent to which the guaranteed life has grown. A 1000-page book—*Encyclopedia of U.S. Government Benefits*[1]—at least hints at this political rampage, and favorably. There are over 500 headings ranging from Aerial Photographs to Zoological Park, from Social Security to Venereal Disease, and so on. Further, there are many subheadings, particularly under Business Aids, Education, Farming—depressingly lengthy in all!

The above, however, relates only to the federal handouts or "benefits." Bear in mind that there are 78,000 state and local governments, nearly all of them offering variations of the guaranteed life.

What are the destructive promises, the ones that cannot and should not be kept; promises that are a sham, a hoax and a sin? The *Bhagavadgita* states what I believe to be a truthful answer:

> Sin is not the violation of a law . . . or convention . . . but ignorance . . . *which seeks its own gain at the expense of others.*

This truth poses two questions that require answers: (1) What is the nature of this "sinful" ignorance? and (2) What is the gain and at whose expense?

All of us are ignorant in more ways than we can count, but the unawareness of this very fact is the ignorance here at issue. Those who suffer this blight—not knowing that they know not—innocently believe that they can run our lives better than we can—an all-too-common naïveté! Nor can the victims of this sinful ignorance be persuaded that they are wrong. Might as well try to enlighten robots!

---

[1] Wm. H. Wise & Co., Inc., Union City, N.J. Under title in frontispiece: "A Complete, practical and convenient guide to United States Government Benefits available to the people of America. Written by a group of Government Experts. Edited by Roy A. Grisham, Jr. and Paul D. McConaughy."

In any event, these millions comprise the guaranteed life tribe. Their promises, while a hoax, a sham and a sin, are believed by them to be the guidelines to heaven on earth. What if their promises could be kept? All of us, in that event, including these victims of false expectations, would be no more than shadows of a sinful ignorance. Indeed, in all probability we would not be here.

What is the gain these poor souls expect for themselves? They find their greatest glory not in wealth—monetary gain—but in casting others in their images: the do-as-I-say syndrome. Thousands times thousands of them have "solutions" to every conceivable problem:

the energy problem	the farm problem
the pollution problem	the housing problem
the over-population problem	the balance of payment problem
the unemployment problem	the safety problem
the poverty problem	the old-age problem
the health problem	the transportation problem
the banking problem	the urban problem
the rural problem	the education problem
the problem of the South	the immigration problem
the problem of the North	problems ad infinitum!

All "solutions" vary except in one respect: these know-it-alls get laws passed coercively to enforce this and that brainstorm. So much for the "gain."

The above-mentioned "gain" is in the form of power—having one's way over others. As to expense, however, that is monetary in the sense that the goods and services by which we live and prosper are measured monetarily, that is, in dollars. As the guaranteed life increases, the costs of government rise beyond what can be collected by direct tax levies. What is the "solution" by those who sponsor this way of life? Inflation, that is, a dilution of the medium of exchange. As the government creates additional dollars to bid goods and services out of the marketplace, each dollar buys less and less.

Back in California in 1927, my wife spent one dollar each day on food for ourselves and two sons. Lettuce, for instance, 5 cents. Today? Fifty cents! Let the guaranteed way of life go its ridiculous way and eventually we'll wind up as did Germany in 1923 when 5 billion marks wouldn't buy a loaf of bread!

There is yet another expense—the most costly of all—for which there is no yardstick. This cost is in terms of life's greatest value: the freedom to act creatively in whatever way one chooses. Freedom of choice is thus diminished and lost. It should be obvious that these expenses are destructive not only of the good life but of life itself, the perpetrators being as much the victims of this depravity as are others.

Finally, those of us who condemn this greatest of all social evils and who believe in freedom, should make certain that our actions do not contradict our beliefs. If they do, we are contributors to the mess we deplore.

For one of countless examples, observe in the *Encyclopedia* mentioned earlier, the many subheadings under "Aids to Business." Most of these are special privileges sought by avowed believers in the free-market way of life. These businessmen, no less than educators or farmers or others who seek special privileges are a part of the problem—seekers of the guaranteed life!

When one understands the fallacy, the evil, and the consequences of the guaranteed life and its many underpinnings, such as power and special privileges, complete rejection will follow. So, the challenge before us is to gain and share this understanding.

The guaranteed life not only is not free—*it is as far from being safe as man can get!*

10

THE FOLLY
OF COMPULSION

Compulsion is contrary to nature.
—QUOTED BY ARISTOTLE

If it were obvious to Aristotle that compulsion is contrary to nature, why is it not obvious to more of us? For if it were obvious, then the number of us who act contrary to nature might decline. That's reason enough to reflect on this most serious of all social matters.

In psychopathology, compulsion is defined as *"an irresistible impulse to perform some irrational act."* In the pathology of our everyday life there are numerous examples of compulsory programs, such as food stamps, Social Security, price control, wage and hour fixing, tariffs, the Gateway Arch, on and on.

How many irrational acts are invading our society today? Count—if you can!—the persons who are advocating compulsion for this or that type of special privilege and then multiply them by the number of compulsions they sponsor—from one to hundreds—and there's the answer. Compulsions by the millions, a massive affront to nature.

Aristotle was unquestionably correct when he said that compulsion is contrary to nature. And no one, to my knowledge, ever commented on nature more brilliantly than Goethe:

Nature understands no jesting; she is always true, always serious, always severe; she is always right, and the errors and faults are always those of man. The man incapable of appreciating her she despises and only to the apt, the pure, and the true, does she resign herself and reveal her secrets.[1]

Goethe used the term "nature" as virtually synonymous with God (righteousness), as had Spinoza before him. Compulsion, therefore, is contrary to the highest we know—against the will of God!

It is self-evident that irrational acts are spawned by irresistible impulses. If the perpetrators could resist such impulses, no doubt they would do so! The reason they cannot resist is that they lack the insight and foresight to see where their own interests lie. These unknowing ones see as gains whatever they compulsorily take from others, abysmally ignorant of the fact that this procedure must eventually lead to impoverishment of themselves and everyone else.

All "gains" by the compulsive political process—like an act of looting—result first in losses to the victims—those from whom taken. But matters do not stop there. When governments start the processes of redistribution, certain consequences follow. Up go the costs of government beyond what can be collected by direct tax levies; inflation ensues; the dollar buys less and less. Merely witness what's going on right now in this and other countries. For a striking example of inflation and its consequences, there is the example of Germany after World War I. By August 1923, five billion marks wouldn't buy a loaf of bread!

Were these irrational persons attuned to nature and guided by enlightened self-interest, they would realize that those individuals gain most who serve best. Receiving and giving—reciprocity—are two sides of the same economic and moral coin. Were they gifted with this understanding, they would not be impelled to perform irrational acts. And how much better off the whole citizenry would be!

Compulsion, the worst of all social follies stems of course from foolish acts of individuals—actions contrary to nature. Goethe's observations about nature, if understood, will enlighten any of us who wish to learn. Here follows my attempt to grasp his insights.

●————————

[1] From Johann Peter Eckermann's *Conversations with Goethe.*

Nature understands no jesting—A jest is "a mocking or bantering remark." And a jester is "a professional fool employed by a ruler in the Middle Ages to amuse him with antics, tricks, jokes."

Must we go back to the Middle Ages for examples of jesting? Antics, tricks, jokes are as rife today as then! Observe our own political rulers and the professionals they employ to amuse the masses with double talk and folderol. And the rulers, no less than the masses, are amused, and for the identical reason: they don't know any better! To them it is a way of life.

Today's mass media are jammed with mocking or bantering remarks—jest, in the worst sense.

If one falls in step with these jesters, then there is no attunement with nature, with righteousness, with Creation. Nature—the will of God—*tolerates* no jesting.

She is always true, always serious, always severe—All truth has its source in nature—Creation. We do not know all that Creation is, but we do know *that* it is. The best we are capable of, with our finite awareness, is to acknowledge Infinite Wisdom as the whole Truth and nothing but the Truth.

Taking one's self too seriously is fraught with danger. But not to take nature seriously is to deny Creation; it is to deaden that quality which responds to, and draws one toward, Infinite Wisdom.

Always severe? Indeed! As already noted, compulsions—acts contrary to nature—result in inflation and, thus, mass poverty. There is no escape. There are countless examples, more than we'll ever know, of how severe are the penalties of defying nature's immutable laws. For instance, defy the law of gravitation by jumping off a tall building! Kersplosh! And if that isn't severe, pray tell, what is!

She [Nature] is always right, and the errors and faults are always those of man—It is easily demonstrable that the more one knows the more he knows he does not know. Why? Nature—Infinity—has no boundary, thus, is beyond human comprehension. The more one knows, the greater is his exposure to the unknown or incomprehensible.

But an awareness of infinity is possible. How? By becoming aware that we cannot even comprehend finite space, a point in space beyond which there is no space. Or a point in time beyond which there is no time!

Approach the problem mathematically. Take the integer one. There is no point beyond which another one cannot be added. The same applies to the infinitesimal. Divide the integer one: 1/2, 1/4, on and on. There will never be a fraction so small that is not divisible.

Is it any wonder that nature—Infinite Wisdom—is always right and that the faults and errors are always those of finite man!

The man incapable of appreciating her she despises—The word "despises" bothers me. Nature which is always right—Righteousness—does not despise. I suspect that the translator of Eckermann's *Conversations* from German to English used a word that has different implications than Goethe had in mind. Perhaps "disregards" was meant, for that makes sense.

Who, then, are incapable of appreciating nature? The victims of the greatest of all faults and errors: the notion, seemingly on the increase, that there is nothing beyond their finite minds. *The infallible I!* Call it egotism or atheism or what you will. Were a speck of dust to compare itself to a galaxy, the comparison would be just as absurd. Nature disregards—passes by—such absurdities!

Only to the apt, the pure, and the true, does she resign herself and reveal her secrets—The apt, the pure, and the true—what a glorious combination of virtues!

The apt: "quick to learn or understand."
The pure: "free from sin or guilt."
The true: "the rightful, faithful."

I shall conclude by quoting Adam Smith, that remarkable individual to whom nature did resign herself and reveal her secrets to an extent seldom recorded:

The statesman who should attempt to direct private people in what manner they ought to employ their capitals would not only load himself with a most unnecessary attention, but assume an authority which could safely be trusted, not only to no single person, but to no council or senate whatever, and *would nowhere be so dangerous as in the hands of a man who had folly and presumption enough to fancy himself fit to exercise it.*

Compulsion is contrary to nature; it is hostile to human liberty. My prayer is that the understanding of liberty and faith in free men may so develop that government will be limited to keeping the peace and invoking a common justice. Then, and not before, will the unimaginable wisdom of the free and unfettered market prevail to bless each and every one of us.

Then and not before will nature, on a grand scale, resign herself and reveal her secrets.

11

WHY NOT SEPARATE SCHOOL AND STATE?

Power tends to corrupt, and absolute power corrupts absolutely.

—LORD ACTON

The question I wish to pose, and seek to answer, is this: Does government—organized force—have any more rightful role to play in education than in religion? The sage observation by Lord Acton (1834–1902) is really the key to my thesis, a point to be explained below. Should the answer turn out to be negative, which I believe it will, then we are faced with another question: What are the appropriate methods for changing the well-nigh overwhelming sentiment to the contrary? To challenge public (government) education in this day and age is akin to denouncing motherhood, the former as popularly sacrosanct as the latter.

Most thinking people will admit that the separation of Church and State was a forward step in Western Civilization. Yet, few there are who have the slightest idea of the name of the scholar mainly responsible for the initial separation; nor do they know the time of its occurrence, the ideological antagonisms of this medieval period, or the tactics used by the State Church to preserve its political dictatorship.

My own meager knowledge of these matters derives from a book first published in 1910, authored by Andrew Dickson White:

Seven Great Statesmen.[1] White was a professor of history at the University of Michigan, later co-founder and president of Cornell University, and known to freedom devotees of our time for his great book *Fiat Money Inflation in France.*[2]

White accords first place among his seven statesmen to Paolo Sarpi, a Venetian priest. White declares that Sarpi

> . . . fought the most bitter fight for humanity ever known in any Latin nation, and won a victory by which the whole world has profited ever since.

This "bitter fight" took place in the late 16th and early 17th centuries, and repercussions were felt all over Europe.

The ideological antagonism was between Venice and the Roman Court: The Papal Establishment. Venice was far more than the city we know today; it was the trading center of the world—freedom in trade more nearly approached than ever before in history. As to the opposition, White points out, it was founded on:

> . . . a theocratic theory, giving the papacy a power supreme in *temporal* as well as in *spiritual* matters throughout the world.

In view of the fact that Catholicism was as much respected by the Venetians as by the Romans, the issue was not religious. Rather, it was political: independence—to trade or whatever—versus a dictatorship encompassing matters social as well as spiritual.

Vicious? Of earlier papal dictators, as distinguished from many remarkable Popes *once Church and State were separated,* White reports:

> The Venetian Ambassadors [to Rome] were the foremost in Europe. . . . They saw Innocent III buy the papacy for money. They had been at the Vatican when Alexander VI had won renown as a secret murderer. They saw, close at hand, the merciless cruelty of Julius II. They had carefully noted the crimes

---

[1] New York: The Century Co., 1919.
[2] Irvington, N.Y.: The Foundation for Economic Education, Inc., 1959.

of Sixtus IV, which culminated in the assassination of Julian de' Medici beneath the dome of Florence. . . . They had sat near Leo X while he enjoyed the obscenities of the *Calandria* and the *Mandragora*,—plays which, in the most corrupt of modern cities, would, in our day [1910], be stopped by the police. No wonder that, in one of their dispatches, they speak of Rome as "the sewer of the world."

Move on to the year 1607. The Papal *political* Establishment, keenly aware that a lone individual—Sarpi—was its nemesis, the threat to a continuing dictatorship, decided to get rid of him. White, after carefully researching this lowest form of having one's way, reports:

> On a pleasant evening in October, 1607, a carefully laid trap was sprung. Returning from his day's work at the Ducal Palace, Father Paul [Sarpi], just as he had crossed the little bridge of Santa Fosca . . . was met by five assassins . . . these ruffians sprang upon him in the dusk, . . . gave him fifteen dagger thrusts . . . and then, convinced that they had killed him, fled to their boats. . . .

Surprisingly, Sarpi survived and, fortunately for Western Civilization, he was able to put the final touches on that brilliant reasoning of his which led eventually to a separation of Church and State!

Reflect now on Lord Acton's dictum: "Power tends to corrupt, and absolute power corrupts absolutely." This profound observation is quoted now and then, but rare indeed is the individual who grasps its significance. Were I asked to name the number one human frailty most responsible for the woes of mankind and the archenemy of individual liberty, power would be it. Friedrich von Hayek, in his book *The Road to Serfdom,* expanded on this thought in a chapter entitled "Why The Worst Get On Top."[3]

Who are "the worst" in society, as Hayek sees it? Power mongers, precisely the same breed as Lord Acton—a devout Catholic—warned against: those who seek power in order to cast others in their blighted

---

[3] Chicago: The University of Chicago Press, 1967, pp. 134–152.

images. Anyone who tends or even wishes to exercise power over others is tainted, and those who gain absolute power are wholly debased! Briefly, they are those who lack the common sense to mind their own business; they strive—with varying degrees of success—for dictatorial power over your life and mine.

There would be little need to dwell on this matter if the power mongers corrupted only themselves. Were they alone to fail in expanding their own awareness, perception, consciousness—life's purpose—we could bemoan their plight and let it go at that. But observe how their corruption wreaks havoc on the rest of us!

Simply stated, man is a social as well as an individualistic being. As individuals we are all unique, no two remotely alike. We live by working with and for each other. Each individual produces and exchanges the fruits of his uniqueness, in the form of goods, services, and ideas. This is the social side. Now to my point: To the extent that the power mongers get their way, to that extent are we made dummies—our uniqueness squelched! Reflect on the mess they make by this maneuver: The schemes of those who don't even know they know nothing are *substituted for the potential creativity of the countless millions.*

Properly defined, absolute power takes the form of aggressive, coercive, physical force. A few have perceived what Lord Acton observed. Socrates possessed that rare wisdom which removed any tendency for power:

I know nothing but I know that I know nothing.

Shakespeare observed the results of power:

Man, proud man! dressed in a little brief authority, plays such fantastic tricks before high heaven as make the angels weep.

So did John Foster Dulles:

Dictatorships usually present a formidable exterior. They seem, on the outside, to be hard, glittering, and irresistible. Within, they are full of rottenness.

Power to rule the lives of others is doubtless a far more common ambition than the desire for riches. All history seems to attest to this. Nor does it make one whit of difference what posts are occupied by power mongers: *religious, political, or educational.* Allow absolute power to the Papal Establishment and the power mongers will crowd out the spiritually minded.

Parenthetically, those individuals who qualify as the cream of mankind are never observed in positions of coercive power over others. Why? It isn't that the masses would reject them, but rather that such persons would never accept dictatorship over a single individual—let alone over a village or state or nation or the world. Each realizes that he himself is the only person among all who live that he has been commissioned to reform and improve—that this is the biggest project Infinite Wisdom has assigned to anyone!

Apply similar considerations to schooling and I cannot help but draw this conclusion: Allow absolute power to the Educational Establishment and power mongers will become our "teachers."

Have a look at what we call "public education" or "free education." Free? The taxpayers foot the bill, a very high amount per student per year.

Government "education" includes three forms of coercion: (1) compulsory attendance, (2) government-dictated curricula, and (3) the forcible collection of the wherewithal to pay the enormous bill.

True, our "educational" power mongers are more sophisticated, or should we say less obviously brutal, in getting their way than were medieval "Popes." But, Mr. Taxpayer, refuse to pay the bill and see what happens! Try it if you wish to find out; I won't!

The results of force are bad enough as related to the pocketbook, but they are far worse as they affect the educational process. Force is precisely as inefficacious in education as when applied to religion and for the same reason. Merely look about and observe the countless thousands of "teachers" who cannot read or write in the realm of ideas; indeed, many of them cannot even get a good grade in spelling! Reflect on this lamentable situation:

- Coercion is a ramming-into procedure. Education is a taking-from process.

- "Graduation" in many schools requires no more than attendance; learning is no longer a criterion.

- To really appreciate the extent of coercion, try to run a private school and observe how your freedom of choice and action is restricted. The power mongers insist that you run your school their way—no other. This coercion—backed by physical force, the constabulary—is rapidly on the increase.

So I ask, why not separate School and State as Church and State are now separated? Leave education to the free market where the wisdom is. Let organized force—government—have no role, none whatsoever, other than to inhibit fraud and misrepresentation.[4]

Finally, we face the challenge as to how such a formidable, seemingly impossible, wholly unpopular task can be achieved. A fact in our favor is that this is not a numbers problem. Father Paul—Sarpi—proved that. Further, such an objective is not to be attained by combative methods. Father Paul confined himself to pure reason, having many freedom devotees in Venice who were capable of seeing the light he shed and who stood steadfastly in his support. The victory!

For a remarkable illustration of how the separation of Church and State worked its wonders, observe how diametrically different was Leo XIII (Pope, 1878–1903) than were the power mongers 300 years earlier, prior to Sarpi's victory. Wrote this wise Pope:

> It is the mind, or reason, which is the predominant element in us who are human creatures; it is this which renders a human being human, and distinguishes him essentially and generically from the brute.

Here we have wisdom of the highest order, for it is reason that distinguishes human beings from the brutes—the power mongers. Let even a few among us resort to reason, and brutishness—murder, war, coercive "education," and the like—will be no more than historical nightmares. And then? We will witness mankind in freedom pursuing human destiny: *Ascendancy!*

---

[4] I have given my analysis as to where lies the responsibility for the child's education, plus a critique of government education as well as the case for free-market education—Chapters 15, 16, 17—in *Anything That's Peaceful*, pp. 180–221.

12
ASLEEP AT
THE SWITCH

When they are asleep you cannot tell a good man from a bad one.

—ARISTOTLE

The metaphor, "asleep at the switch," means "not alert to a duty or opportunity," the sense in which it is here used.

No one remembers falling asleep! The moment of dropping off is lost to us; we only remember coming awake—if indeed we ever do awake! As to duties and opportunities unlimited—no person has awakened to more than an infinitesimal few of them. Those of us now asleep at the switch either have never awakened or, if temporarily aroused by this or that, have since lost interest and fallen back into a lifelong slumber. This appears to explain why so many of us are dead to the world of wonders, to the exciting duties and opportunities of our earthly existence.

When it comes to liberty, all but a few are asleep at the switch, dead to this remarkable wonder that opens the door to opportunities unlimited. Why this plight? What should we do about it? These questions need serious examination.

John W. Burgess maintained that mankind did not begin with liberty but, rather, that mankind acquires liberty through civilization. Liberty is but the flowering of human ascendancy in virtues and principles. The first known civilization emerged in Sumer about 5,000 years ago. Liberty, as we think of it, was no more in the minds of earlier mankind than the free market or private property or limited government or air conditioning or harnessed electric energy or millions of recent phenomena. Prior to Sumer, mankind had not become civilized enough to acquire liberty.

A civilized person, according to my ideal, must recognize that man is at once a social and an individualistic being. Thus, he must not only be self-responsible but, at the same time, understand that he owes to others no infringements on their rights.

In a word, the truly civilized person is a devotee of freedom; he opposes all man-concocted restraints against the release of creative human energy.

The civilized person realizes how incorrect it is to think of freedom as synonymous with unrestrained action. Freedom does not and cannot include any action, regardless of sponsorship, which lessens the freedom of a single human being. To argue contrarily is to claim that freedom can be composed of freedom negations, patently absurd. Unrestraint carried to the point of impairing the freedom of others is the exercise of license not freedom. To minimize the exercise of license is to maximize the area of freedom.

Ideally, that is, in a civilized society, government would restrain license, not indulge in it; make it difficult, not easy; disgraceful, not popular. A government that does otherwise is licentious, not liberal— and a people who permit this are not quite civilized.

To illustrate uncivilized actions: Those in "the Third World," that is, the people in the impoverished or underdeveloped countries, with a few notable exceptions, are asleep at the switch. As a consequence they starve by the millions. Asleep to what? Not only to how the free and unfettered market works its wonders but also to the reasons why government should be limited. They are miserable. That's one side of the uncivilized coin.

The other side is just as uncivilized. American politicians observe the plight of these people. Their conclusion: "We must save them!" By demonstrating how to overcome their poverty? By teaching them how to save and accumulate capital and to freely trade and compete? No, for these dictocrats haven't the slightest idea themselves as to this, the only remedy. They are unaware of the differences between liberty and slavery. So, what is their solution? Confiscation! They *coercively* acquire dollars by the hundreds of billions, every dollar taken from the fruits of our labors and *gratuitously* passed on to these victims of underdevelopment. By any reasonable definition, such action is uncivilized. Merely bear in mind that mankind acquires liberty through civilized actions, and it is obvious that such giveaway programs destroy the very foundations of liberty.

Examples abound of smaller but comparable "programs" emanating from federal, state, and local governments. Observe this sequence:

1. Governments, having no money of their own, must first coercively take away in order gratuitously to give away.

2. That which is coercively taken away is the source of our livelihood.

3. There cannot be life without livelihood.

4. To the extent that livelihood is taken, to that extent are citizens deprived of life.

5. These deprivations diminish individual liberty—liberty being the flowering of civilized individuals.

6. Give-away "programs" quite obviously put the cart before the horse—cause and effect in reverse.

7. Those thus engaged are not awake to the duties and opportunities liberty opens to human beings. They are, indeed, asleep at the switch!

Of the two questions to be answered the first is, why this devastating plight? Why are so many dead to the wonders of liberty? These persons cannot remember falling asleep. Perhaps they never were awake and, thus, are sound asleep to mankind's high purpose—individual evolution and the liberty to act creatively as one pleases. They are in the same plight as were the ancients prior to Sumer, the first known civilization. Nor should we be surprised at this seeming delinquency, and for at least two reasons:

1. Evolution is a very slow process, gracing only a relative few since Cro-Magnon man of some 35,000 years ago.

2. Were we to collapse the eons of time since life first appeared into a single year—a comprehensible span of time—human liberty had its inception only 3½ seconds ago. It is the newest of all politico-economic concepts, opening the way to duties and opportunities: creation at the human level. Little wonder that only a few have the slightest idea as to what liberty is all about. The millions—and understandably—asleep at the switch!

There are, of course, numerous levels or depths of sleepiness. They range from sound asleep to drowsiness to catnaps to half awake. By the same token, awareness of liberty ranges from zero to brief glimmers to rather profound understanding.

What do people do when asleep? A few are sleepwalkers but, mostly, they do no more than *dream*. And a dream, as related to this thesis, is a pipe dream: "a fantastic idea, vain hope, or impossible plan. . . ." I must conclude, therefore, that all the "plans" or any fraction thereof which are inconsistent with civilized actions—the fountain of liberty—are no more than thrusts from primitive antiquity. They are *imagined* utopias or paradises—various forms of Shangri-La!

Wrote Goethe: "None are more hopelessly enslaved than those who falsely believe they are free." The millions who are asleep at the switch and who dream and unknowingly pave the road to their own slavery actually think they are as free as the few who are partially awake and have some understanding of liberty. The millions who falsely believe they are free are enslaved by a dreadful ignorance: *not knowing their plight but not knowing that they know not!* Attempts to sell liberty to these millions are as fruitless as trying to sell a course in physical fitness to a corpse.

The second question would seem to be, what are *we* to do about this plight? However, this is neither a *we* nor a *wee* problem. Instead, it is an *I* and an *Infinite* problem.

What, then, am I to do? Spend my time and energy trying to awaken those who are asleep at the switch as most freedom devotees are doing? Or, shall I take that seldom-traveled uphill road that leads to my own awakening? These are my choices; it's one or the other! My decision to take the latter course is founded on several observations.

1. Who among all the people inhabiting this earth have I been commissioned to save? Only yours truly, an answer with which no one will disagree. Try to find an individual in this or any other country who believes my role is that of his savior. Not one, and that's the way it should be!

2. What if I were to take the other course—awaken a person asleep at the switch? What is his reaction to being yelled at, to setting him straight? "Get off my back!" "Shut up!" "Leave me alone!" "Mind your own business!" "Who do you think you are?" These reforming tactics spawn adversaries and antagonists, never friends or seekers of one's light. Again, this is the way it should be. Erroneous methods only multiply existing errors.

3. What is the right method? Rather than wasting one's energy vainly trying to improve others, it is *to better one's self!* Why is this a civilizing procedure that spawns liberty? Because coming awake to liberty is exclusively a personal achievement. Human betterment in this aspect of life has as many points of origin as there are human beings. I cannot originate improvement in you or you in me.

4. Wrote Edmund Burke: "Example is the school of mankind; they will learn at no other." This wise observation applied no less to Burke or Socrates or Emerson than it relates to you and me.

Merely note how many of us still seek the tutorship of these seers, and of numerous other individuals who have been and are way out front in their intellectual, moral, and spiritual enlightenment. Those who seek truth are attracted to exemplars. All history attests to this law of attraction—the drawing power of excellence. The school of mankind to which Burke refers issues no degrees and has no graduates. It is, instead, perpetual progression—self-dedication for life!

The few who really count in advancing civilization and liberty are those who are alert not only to their duties but to opportunities unlimited. They are those rare persons not asleep at the switch. May their tribe increase, for your sake and mine!

13

QUOTH THE RAVEN "EVERMORE"

For men may come and men may go,
But I go on for ever.

—TENNYSON

Suppose you were one of those who seek public acclaim as an "intellectual." How would you proceed? Would you not contrive brief, catchy phrases, slogans, and the like which appeal to the millions who do no thinking for themselves, jingles which invite repetition? The aim would be to "sell the masses" on a notion or a program. In the politico-economic realm we hear such clichés as "Tax the rich to help the poor" or "One man's gain is another's loss" or "You can't eat freedom," sad sayings over and over again—packaged to sell.

Let us now shift to the poetic realm. Why? Because I wish to try a reverse twist or a different application of Edgar Allan Poe's famous fable in verse, *The Raven*. Poe wrote an 11-page analysis of how he went about the construction of the poem. He had one aim and one only: *"universally appreciable."* In a word, something saleable! To achieve this he had his narrator featured by sadness. In response to each forlorn hope, the Raven would repeatedly croak, "Nevermore"—sadness packaged to sell! Here is the penultimate—the 17th—stanza:

"Be that word our sign of parting, bird or fiend!"
   I shrieked, upstarting,
"Get thee back into the tempest and the Night's
    Plutonian shore!
Leave no black plume as a token of that lie thy
    soul hath spoken!
Leave my loneliness unbroken!—quit the bust above
    my door!
Take thy beak from out my heart, and take thy form
    from off my door!"
           Quoth the Raven, "Nevermore."

Poe's narrator was praying for surcease. Unlike our present-day seekers after truth, he sought only relief from the torturing memory of his lost Lenore. In his tormented musings, he fancies the bird is still perched above his chamber door, looking down at him with eyes that have "all the seeming of a demon's that is dreaming." And he begs the bird: "Leave my loneliness unbroken, quit the bust above my door." To which the Raven (i.e., the narrator's searing memory and grief) croaks a hopeless "Nevermore."

Poe touched here on a profound and universal circumstance; for the seeker after truth often experiences pain at its final discovery. Long-held dogmas are called in question. Old shibboleths are violated. Among the wraiths of dying error, there is always a "lost Lenore." The birth of an idea, no less than that of a human infant, is a painful process. Nevertheless, the pain must be endured if life is to continue, and if truth is to live. Far better, then, that he for whom new light is dawning should modify (and, if necessary, mangle) Poe's lines to read:

"Flaunt a white plume as a token of the truth
    that has been spoken;
I am bowed but never broken when the old
    things fall away.
Keep me ever seeking, turning to the
    light of newer learning
Thrust thy beak within my heart, and make me
    search for truth today . . .
           And **EVERMORE!**"

The narrator's dilemma was sadness and hopelessness, nothing aglow for the future, life's mission in the past tense. That's why Poe had the raven repeat, "Nevermore."

My mission and vision is precisely the opposite: one of happiness and hopefulness. This is why my Raven crows a hopeful, "Evermore."

One participant at a recent seminar remarked, "That's the best lecture I have every heard; it hurts but it's true." A long-held dogma, an old socialistic shibboleth, down the drain! Of course it hurt. One cannot part with a notion held supreme without mental pain. But a seeker of enlightenment, as is this man, is happy with a newly discovered truth. Of such persons it can be said, "Hope springs eternal in the human breast." Fortunately, my outlook is precisely the same as that of Tennyson's brook:

> For men may come and men may go,
> But I go on for ever.

Why? Mine is a commanding ambition: To achieve an ever-improving understanding and exposition of human freedom. Such a goal is far above the mundane affairs of men and borders on the celestial. To make even a minor contribution requires that I go on forever. But the journey is a happy one. Like the brook, I pass scenes of beauty and of challenge:

> By thirty hills I hurry down
> Or slip between the ridges;
> By twenty thorps, a little town,
> And half a hundred bridges.

Freedom, as I define the term—no man-concocted restraints against the release of creative human energy—has been approximated only a few times in the history of man. And, then, for relatively short periods. Otherwise, what has been the human situation? Long-held dogmas, old shibboleths, authoritarianism—one "lost Lenore" after another.

Finally, not the slightest progress can be made toward such a goal unless the quest is featured by happiness. Have fun or forget it! Keep in mind Goethe's truth: "Miracle is the darling child of faith."

Have faith—hopefulness—or forget it!
  The above way of life is why I say to my Raven:

    "Thrust thy beak within my heart, and make me
      search for truth today—and *Evermore!*"

●────────────

My gratitude to Ralph Bradford. While this soliloquy was my idea, numerous thoughts and phrasings and the modified Raven are his. I am not a poet and know it!

14
THIS TIDE OF
UNREASON

Let us not dream that reason can ever be popular.
Passions, emotions, may be made popular, but
reason remains ever the property of the few.

—GOETHE

For striking evidence that reason is less popular than are passions and
emotions, read a book by Andrew Dickson White, a professor of
history at the University of Michigan and later co-founder and first
President of Cornell University. One of his specialties was the French
Revolutionary period and its monetary nonsense.

White, as President of Cornell, delivered a speech entitled, "Fiat
Money Inflation in France," before the Senate and the House of the
U. S. Congress. The next day, April 13, 1876, he repeated it at the
Union League Club, New York City. This scholar and diplomat
continued to study and elaborate on that speech and in 1912 it
appeared as a small book by that same title and "for private use only."
A new edition was issued by the Los Angeles Chamber of Commerce
in the early forties when I was General Manager, and numerous
printings have been undertaken by FEE.[1]

---

[1] Available in paperback from FEE.

What follows is a commentary on a single paragraph from White's book which, if carefully reflected upon, has a lesson for the few who reason:

> Singular, that the man who stood so fearlessly against *this tide of unreason* has left to the world simply a reputation as the most brilliant cook that ever existed!

The man referred to was Brillat-Savarin (1755–1826). This French-man lived in Bresse, a rich and fertile region in eastern France. He was, as any well-read gastronome will concede, the founder of modern cooking. Of his numerous talents, this art was his lifetime love. Not only was he the ingenious innovator of countless, delectable dishes but he spent his adult life putting his recipes into instructive, witty words and phrasings. His book, *La Physiologie de goût*, was released in 1825, a year before he passed away.

Mrs. M. F. K. Fisher, a distinguished writer and cook herself, translated the innovative work of this Frenchman into English, published as *The Physiology of Taste*.[2] Not only have I read the book but I have dined in Bresse where I savored Poularde de Bresse en Crème—one of Brillat-Savarin's recipes and what a chicken dish!

Brillat-Savarin was an innovative, inventive genius of the culinary art—a bright star in his field, comparable to Edison and Kettering in theirs. And, like these two inventors, he was a true devotee of the freedom way of life. Further, this star of my theme was also a lawyer, an economist, and a member of the National Assembly during the French Revolutionary period.

It was during this period that Mirabeau, a great orator and hero of the masses, urged yet another enormous issue of assignats—paper money "secured" by confiscated Catholic church properties, which comprised more than one-fourth of all the land in France. Of course, the assignats were irredeemable legal tender, as is our paper currency.

Brillat-Savarin, responding to Mirabeau's proposal, "called attention to the depreciation of assignats already felt. He tried to make the Assembly see that *natural laws work as inexorably in France as*

---

[2] Copyright by The George Macy Companies, Inc., 1949.

elsewhere; he predicted that if this new issue were made, there would come a depreciation of thirty per cent." White then refers to Brillat-Savarin as "the man who so fearlessly stood against *this tide of unreason.*"

Right now we in the U.S.A. are faced with a tide of unreason on the rampage. Natural law works as inexorably here as in France or elsewhere; our legal tender, like the assignats of yore, is suffering the same fate and for the same reason: passions, emotions, expediency. As did Mirabeau, many know better but yield to temptation—popular or political. Spineless!

Thank heaven, there are the few, in and out of office, who, as Brillat-Savarin, stand against our tide of unreason. Goethe was so right: ". . . reason remains ever the property of the few."

The question is, will our few exemplars stand as models for future generations? Will their righteousness grace not only this generation but also our progeny? The answer is assuredly affirmative, for every action—good or evil—casts its light or darkness into the days and months and years ahead, dwindling or intensifying as time goes on.

Brillat-Savarin's righteousness—"the man who so fearlessly stood against this tide of unreason"—was no more sacrosanct than the righteousness of a few others in the National Assembly. Yet, the glorious stature of those others is all but forgotten—dwindled away—while his example is still aglow, a light in today's darkness. Why his and not the others? Answer this question and the few righteous ones of our time will possess a guideline to brighten the lives of future generations.

I feel certain that Andrew Dickson White would no more have singled out—highlighted, dramatized—Brillat-Savarin than one or two others in the National Assembly had it not been for that Frenchman's *excellence* as an innovator of cooking and his consequent reputation as a gastronomical genius. A reputation for excellence in any one of countless fields carries with it a drawing power; it attracts listeners not only in one's own time but into the future.

Observe the tendency of the masses to accept any opinion voiced by those who have the reputation of being the greatest in any one endeavor, be it football, baseball, or whatever. For instance, there are virtuosic orators such as Cicero, or William Jennings Bryan, or some other. Millions listened to them in their time and ever so many know of their messages today. And it makes not one whit of difference whether or not the ideological views be buncombe or wisdom. A reputation for excellence has an unbelievable thrust to it, regardless of wisdom or nonsense.

Finally, what does this mean for our few who stand ramrod straight for the private ownership, free market, limited government way of life? If their ideas are to bear fruit in the future and have more attraction than the famous who father babble and ignoble notions, they must gain a reputation for excellence. Let it be in oratory or writing or fearlessness or cooking or whatever most nearly approximates their uniqueness.

As Goethe wrote, ". . . reason can never be popular." Nor can being right! May our few who achieve excellence side with Henry Clay: "I would rather be right than be president." President Lincoln gave us a good guideline to achieve excellence:

Let us have a faith that right makes might, and in that faith, let us to the end, dare to do our duty, as we understand it.

15

IGNORANCE: AGENT OF DESTRUCTION

There is nothing more terrible than igno-rance in action.

—GOETHE

As Victor Hugo observed, "Armies can be resisted." Indeed, they can! But what about bad ideas, that is, ignorance? The most difficult problem facing the people of the United States today is to resist ignorance in action.

Were I a loyal Russian devoted to the U.S.S.R.—Union of Soviet *Socialist* Republics—and determined to overcome, subvert, and absorb the U.S.A., what would my tactic be? Drop hydrogen bombs? Probably not! That tactic would be resisted as would an invading army. What then? Would I not try to outmaneuver resistance by attractively phrasing and propagandizing the ideas of socialism? I'd play upon such themes as "From each according to his ability, to each according to his need." How would I measure my success? By the extent to which the people of the United States adopted my creed, the ten points of the *Communist Manifesto*.

As a devotee of freedom, thus opposed to compulsory collec-tivism, I view with distress the extent to which Americans have embraced the ten points. Here are substantially accurate assessments:

1. *Abolition of property in land and application of all rents of land to public purposes*—Our 78,000 governmental units—federal, state, and local—own outright not less than 39 percent of all acreage. And the remaining land in private title is only partially owned, for government may exert eminent domain over it, and no one owns that which he does not control. To public purposes? Who knows, except it is enormous![1]

2. *A heavy or progressive* income tax—Complete acceptance!

3. *Abolition of all right of inheritance*—With graduated estate tax rates running as high as 70 percent and state inheritance taxes being added on to that, the right of inheritance appears to be in the twilight zone.

4. *Confiscation of the property of all emigrants and rebels*—The government's shameful treatment of Japanese-Americans during World War II, on the mere suspicion that they might do something to hamper the war effort, was a breach of American standards of justice. Excused as a wartime emergency measure, the precedent nevertheless remains to haunt the nation in times of peace—the rights of people may be suspended any time on the pretext of an "emergency."

5. *Centralization of credit in the hands of the State, by means of a national bank with State capital and an exclusive monopoly*—The Federal Reserve System, together with the legal tender laws, have substantially accomplished this objective.

6. *Centralization of the means of communication and transport in the hands of the State*—The extent to which control of communication and transportation is in the F.C.C. and the I.C.C. tends to reduce the question of formal ownership to the point of insignificance. There is no ownership without control.

7. *Extension of factories and instruments of production owned by the State, the bringing into cultivation of waste lands and the improvement of the soil generally in accordance with a common plan*—The postal system and the T.V.A. are examples of moves in this direction. Government ownership of land noted in point number 1 and recent controls of all kinds applied in the name of consumer

---

[1] For a further and enlightening development of this point, see "Changing Concepts of Private Property" by Bertel M. Sparks (*The Freeman*, October 1971).

protection are others. The entire list is too extensive for coverage in the space available in this article.

8. *Equal liability of all to labor. Establishment of industrial armies, especially for agriculture*—With the federal government controlling the right to hire and fire, as well as the wages being paid, this objective has been substantially accomplished.

9. *Combination of agriculture with manufacturing industries; gradual abolition of the distinction between town and country, by a more equable distribution of the population over the country*— Zoning laws are already controlling land use in most of our urban areas and many rural areas as well. Population shifts are being controlled by denying sellers the right to choose their own customers.

10. *Free education for all children in public schools. Abolition of children's factory labor in its present form*—We have free education in public schools and our child labor laws do, in fact, prohibit children from working in factories. Complete agreement! However, public education is far from free, in Russia or here. It is unbelievably expensive.

What an infestation of communistic ideas! In the politico-economic realm, the U.S.S.R. type of State has nothing above it, thus, the State is God. What constitutes such a State? Individuals politically exercising all-out coercive power. This is quite the opposite of the wisdom on which America's government was founded, namely, that all men are endowed by their Creator—not by the State—with the rights to life and liberty.

There is, however, a common notion among freedom devotees that should be questioned, the notion that this urge for compulsory collectivism has its origin in the Union of Soviet *Socialist* Republics. Their society is but a modern variation on primitive ways of life: serfdom, feudalism, mercantilism, and the like. Their propaganda is cleverly drawn to have us believe theirs is the wave of the future. The communist theoreticians believe their tactics are causing our slump into socialism, as do many Americans, but the belief is erroneous. Our slump, no less than theirs, is but a thrust from the primitive past—in different grammar, that's all!

As to why communistic notions portray ignorance, our Pilgrim Fathers made the discovery during their first three years—1620–1623. During those years they practiced "From each according to his ability, to each according to his need" about 2½ centuries before Marx put the nonsense into words.

Why did these forefathers of ours abandon this practice? They were starving! No intelligence is required to give away food and fabric but to do so presupposes something in the warehouse. Their warehouses were too near empty to sustain life.[2]

What was the cure for this ignorance in action? Governor Bradford and the remaining Pilgrims turned to the wisdom of the market—private ownership, that is, to each according to his productivity. Success attended this wise move, thereby setting the stage for the American miracle!

Unfortunately, an increasing number of Americans—millions of them—have all but forgotten their remarkable heritage, a root of which was the Pilgrim awakening. It is an observed fact that these millions are becoming more and more afraid of and are running away from the American revolutionary concept. What, then, are they running toward? The *Communist Manifesto*, the nonsense from which, the Pilgrims escaped long before Marx advocated it: "From each according to his ability, to each according to his need." The eventual economic by-product? Unless the trend is reversed, it must be empty warehouses!

The trend cannot be reversed unless we discover the causes that are to be avoided and the cure that is to be taken. Such discovery depends upon improved analysis and thinking.

The first cause will come as a shock to most people: *"If you are not a part of the solution, you are a part of the problem."* It is self-evident that those who pay no heed to the present trend—afflicted with complacency—are a part of the problem. They drift with the ideological tide—unknowingly. As a consequence, they vote in accord with the current tide, that is, for the planned economy and the welfare state: socialism, ignorance in action.

The second cause is a lack of awareness of the American heritage or its genesis. People observe socialism advancing and at the same time they experience increased prosperity. Jumping to a false conclusion they attribute their material well-being to the socialism—a

---

[2] See *Of Plymouth Plantation* by William Bradford, edited by Harvey Wish (New York: Capricorn Books, 1962).

seriously mistaken correlation. We are as prosperous as we are only because our productivity is strong enough to carry on *in spite* of the socialistic nonsense.[3] Briefly stated, the genesis of the prosperity we still enjoy is this: The Constitution and the Bill of Rights more severely restrained government action than ever before in history, limiting government to keeping the peace and invoking a common justice. There was a minimum of organized force standing against the release of creative human energy. The result was an unprecedented outburst of creativity—the miracle!

Finally, how does one become a part of the solution? By trying to become an aristocrat as defined by Jefferson: "There is a natural aristocracy among men; it is composed of virtues and talents."

The reason that we are witnessing such an abundance of nonsense in action is a devastating slump in virtues and talents among individuals in all walks of life—religion, education, business, labor or whatever. Nonsense runs rampant whenever the aristocratic spirit is weak and faltering; it is checked, held in abeyance, whenever virtues and talents are rising to set a glorious standard.

Your role and mine? We have no short cut except to exemplify as best we can the aristocratic spirit. Only then does each of us become a *part of the solution!*

----

[3] See "An American Mirage" in my book *Awake for Freedom's Sake.*

16

THE SHOW-OFF
IS WAY OFF

Talent for talent's sake is a bauble and a show. Talent working with joy in the cause of universal truth lifts the possessor to new power as a benefactor.
—EMERSON

Wrote Baltasar Gracián, the Spanish philosopher and satirist two centuries before Emerson:

The larger the number of gifts [talents] the less the need to affect any, for such would be vulgar insult to all of them.

What follows is an attempt to analyze Emerson's and Gracián's thoughts by seeking answers to these questions:

1. Why is the seeking of talent for talent's sake a bauble—"a showy but worthless thing"—or, as Gracián phrased it, "vulgar"?
2. Why does talent working with joy in the cause of universal truth make the practitioner thereof a benefactor?
3. And another point by Gracián: ". . . the man of discrimination will never exhibit his virtues, for it is through their very concealment that they awaken the interest of others." Is it valid?

Talent for talent's sake is no more than a showy and wordy thing; gross if the purpose be vulgar; evil if it be not high. To get away with piracy, thievery, hijacking, embezzlement, and the like takes talent of sorts.

The same can be said about talents aimed at fame, notoriety, or fortune for fortune's sake. And observe the kind of talent so prevalent in the news media—emphasizing the bad to the neglect of the good. Showy stuff!

And above all, note the political talent of getting votes: Say anything to gain or hold office and wield power over the citizenry.

On the other hand is the talent of working with joy in the cause of universal truth—Creation. Those who lead in acquiring and practicing this rare talent are, unquestionably, the highest-ranking benefactors of mankind. These few are capable, to some extent, of intercepting the Divine Intelligence and leading the rest of us in Creation's evolutionary direction. In the absence of such benefactors, mankind would still be at the level of the cave dwellers.

Universal truth, of course, is omnipresent. What unique talent is it that graces our benefactors, enabling them to intercept Truth? It is their preparation, their seeking, their desire to tune in and receive a bit of the Divine Intelligence. This is what lifts a talented one to the new power of a benefactor. Thus graced, each benefactor serves as a go-between, or as Socrates labeled this talent, "a philosophical midwife." They receive from Heavenly sources and share with the few who can tune in and receive their enlightenments.

Emerson speaks of working with joy in the cause of universal truth. This spiritual man, certainly among our benefactors, goes on to explain:

> We lie in the lap of immense intelligence which makes us receivers of its truth and organs of its activity. When we discern justice, when we discern truth, we do nothing of ourselves, but allow a passage of its beams.

This we should try to grasp: to allow a passage of its beams—to intercept the "immense intelligence"—is a skill that manifests itself only if the pursuit of universal truth be joyful. One cannot imagine a complacent or angry person rising to these intellectual, moral, and spiritual heights. As was wisely observed long ago: "Everything that is leavened rises, and joy is the rational elevation or rising of the soul."

The bakers of bread know about leavening. But only now and then do we come upon an individual—past or present—who realizes that the joyous seeking of universal truth is the yeast that determines how much bread—goods and services—shall grace mankind.

Bear in mind that there are two kinds of power—coercive and creative. The practitioners of coercive power are corrupted and degraded. But "talent working with joy in the cause of universal truth lifts the possessor to new power as a benefactor." More power to our benefactors!

Finally, to Gracián's point that the man of discrimination will never exhibit his virtues, *for it is through their very concealment that they awaken the interest of others.* Is it valid? If it is, then most of us devoted to the freedom way of life have a lot of homework to do.

What a show-off I have been in several fields, a virtual exhibitionist! There is an egotistical drive here: flaunting my five holes-in-one, displaying a book and numerous articles by experts proclaiming me a culinary artist, showing off LER's Journal, emphasizing not a missed day in over 26 years, and so on. All of this is, as Emerson asserted, "a bauble and a *show.*" George Elder wrote, "When one talks incessantly about things accomplished, little time is left to do anything."

Suppose I were really a man of discrimination in these areas. What would my method be? Concealment! Shut up! Those who care will awaken and find out anything worth having.

Let a person be a superb golfer. He need not then be a braggart. Everyone interested in that sport will awaken to his skills and his record, holes-in-one or whatever. Further, countless thousands will seek his tutorship.

The same is true in the culinary field. Cook a better meal than others have experienced and they'll ask for your recipes. Concentrate on your cooking, however high your self-esteem. Being a show-off will give your guests a headache, if not a stomachache!

Golf, cooking, and numerous other hobbies of my earlier years have been relegated to second place. Further, because of Gracián's counsel, they'll arouse no more exhibitionism—never again!

What, now, comes first with me? Trying better to understand and explain the freedom philosophy. In this exalted ambition, I am not a show-off. I know next to nothing about it—and know it! And if that be talent, it is well concealed. Yet, as I joyously labor in this vineyard, receiving a thought now and then, improving a word or phrase, drawing on benefactors past and present, thinking of myself as a midwife—not as source—numerous other individuals are awakened and take off on their own.

Gracián's point is, indeed, valid! For evidence, observe so many of the individuals from several walks of life whose avowed aim is to "save free enterprise," and note how they assess themselves: theirs is the last word; they have all the answers—they think! Not the slightest humility or concealment—the omnipotent I! Show-offs and way off!

The main point of this thesis was pronounced 25 centuries ago in the Old Testament book of *Isaiah*. The late Albert Jay Nock wrote a brilliant paraphrase of this wisdom.[1] Those few who really count are unknown—The Remnant. They will have nothing to do with anyone bent on reforming others. Instead, they are awakened and attracted only to those who are seeking light, that is, devoted to their own enlightenment.

Let us then work with joy in the cause of universal truth and acquire that new power which makes us benefactors. By so doing, we will serve Creation at the Heavenly and earthly levels. And that's as high as man can go!

---

[1] See *Notes from FEE*, July 1962, entitled "Isaiah's Job."

17

ON GOING TO EXTREMES

The reverse of error is not truth, but error still.

—RICHARD CECIL

In the physical world there are extremes of heat and cold, of aridity and moisture, north and south, and so on. Then there are perpendicular extremes—up and down; high up into the stratosphere and deep down into the molten rock at the earth's core, extremely deep below the surface.

My aim here is to examine "extremism" in the world of ideas as related to politico-economic behaviors. To use popular terms, ideas range from "left" to "right," that is, from communism, socialism, and the like, to the free-market, private-ownership, limited-government way of life. And, as in the physical world, ideas have their highs and lows—up all the way to heavenly and down all the way to hellish. We live in a world of intellectual as well as physical extremes. An assessment of behavioral extremes is important.

The English divine Richard Cecil (1748–1777), quoted above, says that "the reverse of error is not truth, but error still." This is to say that one might go either forward or backward in error—and two wrongs do not make a right. As related to the politico-economic realm, Cecil's observation is assuredly valid.

At the "left" is socialism which today and throughout history has numerous labels: serfdom, feudalism, mercantilism, Nazism, communism, fascism, the planned economy, the welfare state, the command society—*all-out* government. To appreciate Cecil's point, note the numerous opponents of socialism whose tactic is the advocacy of socialism's opposite—no government at all. Anarchy!

As Ludwig von Mises observed: "Socialism is planned chaos; anarchy is unplanned chaos." Obviously, socialism is erroneous and so is its reverse. Anarchy is not truth, but error still!

If both socialism and anarchy be error, then the notions that spawn them are detrimental to a harmonious society.

First, is socialism a planned, political contrivance? Indeed, yes! The citizens are not permitted to live their lives creatively as they please. Instead, their lives are planned by dictocrats, and the planning is coercively enforced.

Second, does this contrivance result in chaos? Yes! Here are several ways of phrasing the origins of social chaos:

The coercers and the coerced.
The rulers and the ruled.
The human stamping machines and the duplicates.
The be-like-me's and the crude approximations thereof.
The know-nothings with a passion for commanding and those commandeered.

Each infringement upon any one person frustrates the creative self and is chaotic. By definition this is disorder—a disordering of society, naturally harmonious when free.

Was Mises correct in asserting that anarchy is unplanned chaos?

First, is it unplanned? Yes, no political government whatsoever—no social agency—and thus no plan to invoke a common justice or to keep the peace.

True, the anarchists acknowledge their belief in the protection of life and property. However, their "system" is to buy such protection as we buy insurance. It follows that they would have individuals and groups hire their own armed guards. Each residence or business would have its own policeman or corps of cops.

But "protection" is a concept of many colors and much that is done in the cause of "protectionism" involves a governmental or government-like use of coercion to achieve some gain or special privilege for oneself or one's own group. And does anyone believe that merely eliminating government would get rid of powerful labor unions resorting to force to extract wages or conditions of work other than the free market might afford? Or trade associations demanding tariff protection? Or teachers or farmers or candlestick makers or all sorts of business and professional groups demanding their "due"? Or groups of welfare recipients protecting their "rights"? Who is to define or set the limits of unplanned "protection"?

Demonstrations of how anarchy "works" aren't necessary. A bit of diagnostic thinking should suffice. What would be the code of justice? There would be in the U.S.A. 200 million "codes," ranging from that of thieves to the countless millions who seek special privileges, each individual and group using armed force to gain their contradictory ends. Our land would be a battleground, chaos reigning, harmony out of the question. So anarchy is indeed "unplanned chaos."

Socialism is error. Anarchy, its reverse, is error still. It is impossible for these two wrongs to make a right because each is the archenemy of liberty and of man's emergence, evolution, growth.

The term "golden mean" is everywhere defined as the prudent or safe way between two extremes. The ideal—private ownership, free-market, limited-government procedure with its moral and spiritual antecedents—is definitely not halfway between socialism and anarchy. It steps into a different dimension altogether. So, let's call this ideal the *golden mean*, implying the golden way of life which releases individual potential.

The first step in grasping the ideal way of life is to realize that each of us is at once a social and an individualistic being. Discover what aspect is social and all the rest is individualistic.

In what respect are all of us—no exceptions—social beings? *We are interdependent!* Even our forebears who raised most of their own food, built their own shanties, cut their own trees for fuel, did their own weaving, and so on were dependent on others for hammers, saws, stoves, kettles, tea, and numerous other items. My great-great-great-grandfather, who came here prior to the American Revolution, would have perished had self-subsistence been his lot. He, and others of his time, were social beings, each dependent on others—interrelated!

The more specialized we become, the more is our interdependence apparent. For instance, we are now so specialized that I know not how to build my home or raise my food or make my car or my clothes or countless other economic blessings. Talk about a social being! I am so far removed from self-sufficiency that I am *absolutely* dependent upon the free, uninhibited exchange of the little I do—write and lecture—for all the goods and services produced by other millions of social beings. This dependency on one another applies to everyone. If in doubt, reflect upon how well you would prosper were you to live only on that which you now do or know how to do.

Were we to regard this phase of life as individualistic rather than social, that is, attempt the self-sufficient rather than the inter-dependent way, all of us would be starving to death on the periphery of specialization.

It should be self-evident that social beings cannot live life to the fullest unless they are free to exchange their millions of specializations. Primitive barter is obviously unworkable as a means of exchange. For example, we never observe people exchanging a goose for a gallon of gas or office desks for seats on airplanes. Ridiculous!

What then? An economic circulatory system, that is, the medium of exchange—money! And it works automatically with little heed paid to its wondrous performance—*so long as it is honest!* However, as socialism grows and incurs costs far beyond what can be collected by direct tax levies, government resorts to inflation. This dilutes the monetary unit and the dollar—our medium of exchange—is worth less and less, heading toward worthlessness.

Broadly speaking, the above are components that circumscribe the citizenry as social beings. All else is individualistic. In the latter we speak and act for ourselves. But no individual should ever be permitted to speak and act for society; that would be socialism.

In an ideal society, its agency would act on behalf of one and all alike. Ideally, this would be *limited* government, nearly the opposite of what we now have. The agency would be strictly limited as it was following the Declaration of Independence, the Constitution, and the Bill of Rights. The type of social agency that once did and can again grace the lives of Americans is limited to:

Invoking a common justice—no special privilege for anyone.

Keeping the peace, foreign and domestic—let anyone do anything that's peaceful.

Defending against all fraud, violence, predation, misrepresentation—the coercive taking from some and giving to others forbidden.

Freedom to choose, be it occupation, hours of work, goods and services produced, at what prices and to whom sold or exchanged—*laissez-faire*, that is, a fair field and no favoritism.

In the ideal society, government cannot extend welfare or prosperity to this or that group of special-privilege seekers. Why? It is so limited that it has nothing on hand to dispense nor the power to take from some and give to others.

The result? A self-reliant, self-responsible, self-governing citizenry. It was this and this alone which accounted for the unprecedented outburst of creative human energy, the greatest in the world's history, before or since—the *American Miracle!*

The belief that unseated government as sovereign and placed the Creator there? It was the highest wisdom ever written into a political document:

> . . . that all men are . . . endowed by their Creator with certain unalienable Rights, that among these are Life, Liberty and the Pursuit of Happiness.

Let us be done with the extreme of socialism—all-out government—and that too often suggested remedy, the Opposite extreme—anarchy. Socialism is error, and anarchy is error still.

Replace these extremes with the *Golden Mean*, meaning the golden way of life! How go about this?

Merely bear in mind that America's fate does not rest on your or my shoulders—only our heads are there. Our founding fathers used their heads, resulting in a superb nation. May we make it better by carrying our heads proudly high, eyes cast upward, extremely high!

18

THE ROLE OF
SELF-DISCIPLINE

*But man, proud man, Dressed in a little brief
authority, . . .Plays such fantastic tricks before high
heaven as make the angels weep.*

—SHAKESPEARE

Self-discipline, as distinguished from being disciplined by others—
governments, labor unions, neighbors, or whomever—is a necessary
attainment if liberty is to prevail. Self-discipline is a requirement
in every department of life—if life is to be lived at its highest—but
I shall limit the following commentary to this achievement as related
to *responsibility* and *authority.*

Discipline is defined as "training that develops self-control, character, or orderliness and efficiency." These are the elements of self-
discipline, as I shall use the term!

Here's the story of how I came upon the idea that there is a
necessary and proper relationship between responsibility and
authority. In the early forties the Los Angeles Chamber of Commerce,
with myself as General Manager, experienced a far greater success
than like organizations in many large cities. Why did we have
thousands of enthusiastic members and financial supporters while
many business organizations were scrambling for existence? What
were we doing that others were not? After a great deal of pondering,
the answer came to mind.

The L.A. Chamber had 18 departments, each with a manager and staff; 150 people in all. In every instance, when assigning projects to the managers, I gave them not only the responsibility for the undertaking but also the authority to accomplish it. It worked like magic!

Why this procedure? Having had little formal schooling, I was obliged to seek tutors. And from the remarkable Socrates I learned that none of us knows very much. How possibly could the business of Los Angeles County be bettered, I asked myself, if it were but a reflection of my know-nothing-ness! By assigning responsibility and the authority to go with it, the initiative of my 150 associates was tapped; their innovative potentialities bloomed; and the total know-how and energy was tremendous! All of us worked *with* each other, not one in total command, but a happy combination of competition and cooperation.

My predecessor—like most managers of other Chambers—told everybody on his staff what to do and how to do it—period! His do-as-I-say tactic failed to bring out the potential talents of anyone. Thus it was that I chose the working formula: *Delegate responsibility* and *authority commensurately.* This turns out to be the secret of organizational success, be it in Chambers of Commerce, trade associations, business corporations, or even preparing a dinner with your wife. If I say, "Please prepare the salad," I give her the authority to make it her way. As in all other organizational arrangements, she may seek my counsel but the final decision is hers. It works!

Interestingly, it was some 10 years later that I heard this exact phrasing from another. He was the Vice Chairman of perhaps the world's largest corporation, one having many divisions and locations, each with its own president and staff. Responsibility for doing a good job was delegated to each of those presidents along with the authority to accomplish the task. Did it work? One of the greatest corporate successes I have ever known!

As observed earlier, self-discipline, as distinguished from being disciplined by others, is a necessary attainment if liberty is to prevail. And self-discipline significantly relates to both responsibility and authority.

As I have written many times, self-responsibility and liberty are two parts of the same ideological coin. Neither is possible without the other. Nor is self-responsibility possible without a strict self-discipline.

Refusal to turn the responsibility for self over to another or others, which is to relieve self of life's problems, requires a discipline of the highest order. It takes intellectual toughness not to yield to this seductive temptation.

Equally destructive is allowing governments to assume the responsibility for our welfare, deciding for us what we shall learn or produce or with whom exchange or the hours we may work or prices and wages. To thus abandon self-control is a suicidal act. As Verna Hall wrote: "To the extent that an individual turns the responsibility of self over to another or allows government *to take it away, to that extent is the very essence of one's being removed.*"

Next, what about self-discipline as related to authority? Is it necessary? It relates to authority no less than to responsibility. Omission of self-discipline from either one makes it ineffective in the other. It is a double-barreled necessity and unless practiced in both will result in countless disciplines over our lives by governments and other dictocrats.

When one is graced with the responsibility-authority combination—those rare stimulative twins—the chances of success are greatly increased. A person thus graced is head and shoulders above those in comparable endeavors. However, it takes an unusual self-discipline to keep success from going to one's head. The remedy? Acquiring and keeping in mind, day-in-and-day-out, that Socratic truth: *knowing next to nothing!*

At this point, reflect on Shakespeare's wonderfully phrased wisdom: *"But man, proud man, Dressed in a little brief authority, . . . Plays such fantastic tricks before high heaven as make the angels weep."*

Countless individuals gain the reputation of being top *authorities* at this or that bit of expertise—a business or labor tycoon, an economist, a novelist, a writer of communistic doctrine or whatever. They believe as many others do that no one rivals or excels them in their specializations, and perhaps no one does. What is the malady that so often follows these self-assessments? The belief that there is nothing in the Cosmos above their minds! As a consequence, many of them, as Karl Marx, become atheists—their finite minds the Almighty I! Infinite Consciousness—Creation—to them is just so much religious buncombe! Man, proud man! He does, indeed, make the angels weep!

The self-discipline that will remedy such inflated self esteem? No one knows, for it is as indescribable as intuitive flashes or insights having a *Source* which they in their presumed omniscience have denied. From that condition, how does one regain an open mind?

An open mind to what? To the Infinite Unknown! Rarely will those self-designated authorities grasp this concept, for their egotism squelches their reason. Any attempt to deflate their egotism will result (1) in a confirmation of their headiness and (2) in a dislike of all would-be reformers. So what can we do? We can let them go their own way!

Most important, we, too, each of us, can go our own way: strive for humility; acknowledge the mystery of how Creation works its wonders, the wonderful miracle of the free and unfettered market. And we may be grateful to Shakespeare, who warned us against pride, and to Socrates who made it plain to us that the more we know the more we know we do not know.

The role of self-discipline as related to responsibility and authority is to shield us from dictocratic disciplinarians and to assure the liberty that brings peace on earth, good will toward men.

19
━ WHY SEEK THE LIGHT? ━

Light! Nature's resplendent robe; without whose
vesting beauty all were wrapt in gloom.
—EDWARD THOMSON

The following doggerel may serve to dramatize the point here at issue:

There lived two frogs, so I've been told,
In a quiet wayside pool;
And one of these frogs was a blamed bright frog,
But the other frog was a fool.

Now a farmer man with a big milk-can
Was wont to pass that way;
And he used to stop and add a drop
Of the aqua pura, they say.

And it chanced one morn in the early dawn
When the farmer's sight was dim,
He scooped those frogs in the water he dipped,
Which was a joke on him.

The fool frog sank in the swashing tank,
As the farmer bumped to town.
But the smart frog flew like a tugboat screw,
And he swore he would not go down.

So he kicked and splashed and he slammed and thrashed,
And he kept on top through all;
And he churned that milk in first-class shape
In a great big butter ball.[1]

This humorous verse strikingly depicts the human situation in today's U.S.A.

1. There's the farmer who cheats. He obtains the water for free and sells it for milk. Competition? Quite the opposite: the something-for-nothing syndrome! This nicely symbolizes getting paid for not working and the thousand and one other deviations from the private-ownership, free-market, limited-government way of life. In politico-economic affairs, it is an affront to the Golden Rule. Were all to do likewise, all would perish!

2. Then there's the "blamed bright frog." What strength of character can we assign to humans who are similarly oriented? *Never say die!* That frog could not guess what would save his life. He knew less about butter-making than I know about Creation, if that be possible. Even as we mortals, he was unaware what form his salvation would take, or even that he would be saved. But he exemplified a spirit that should feature our lives: *the will to prevail!*

3. And last, the fool frog who, when confronted with an obstacle, behaved as do ever so many humans when faced with cheaters galore: they give up the ghost, throw in the sponge, abandon life's high purpose.

Wrote John Wilmot: "'Tis a meaner part of sense to find a fault than to taste an excellence." This insight requires reflection if its message is to be heeded.

Obviously, it is the better part of wisdom and good sense to seek excellence, and not be constantly *distracted* by the countless faults of mankind. To "taste an excellence"—to seek the right and the good—

[1] Extracted from "Story of a Kicker," by Holman F. Day.

is an objective that should, in my view, feature our mortal moments. To do otherwise is to miss life's golden opportunities. It's a matter of which way the eye be cast—toward the mess we're in or toward the what-ought-to-be; we can choose the darkness or the Light!

The countless faults of mankind are incessantly thrown up at us. Freedom devotees by the tens of thousands allow themselves to be so distracted by the bad that they are blinded to the good—which is thousands of times greater! Merely bear in mind that the eye cannot be cast in opposite directions at the same time.

Why is the bad so blatantly broadcast, causing mass distractions, while the good, ever so much greater, is silent for the most part and has to be sought out? This requires an answer to the question, "What makes news?" The mass media give the answer.

What qualifies as news? Mostly disasters—the bad—only now and then the good—the successes. A jet plane crash is news. Newspapers, TV, radio publicize it the world over. But try to find any reporting on the hundreds of millions of miles flown safely every week. The successful is an un-event: no mention. Hijacking? That's news! Why? It's a disaster—bad and exceptional; but passengers by untold millions have never been hijacked. Is my more than 2,000,000 miles of safe flying news? Indeed not!

A thief robs a bank. News! Millions of citizens day-in-and-day-out, year-in-and-year-out are honest. They promptly pay their bills and keep their promises. *No news!*

This commentary has to do only with the few who are devoted to the freedom philosophy. What destructive tendency has the media on us and what might the remedy be? A strict observation of the correct answer would be a boon to everyone, including freedom's opponents. The following is how I presently see the media's effect and its remedy, though, admittedly, it is a matter of forever probing.

As related to politico-economic affairs, the media, with a few notable exceptions, profusely present the fallacies of socialism as if they were sound. If you listen to radio or TV reporters and commentators or read the daily news or spend time with most weekly and monthly magazines, you listen to and read messages that spell sheer calamity to anyone who understands and believes in human liberty.

Now it may well be that you are one of the exceptional few who can allow such a message of socialism to go in one ear and out the other, shrug it off for the nonsense it is, and let it go at that. In that case, lucky you!

But suppose you aren't one of these lucky few. What happens? *Wholesale distractions* which result in despair, discouragement, pessimism—all is going to pot and ruin! The bad is so overemphasized that the good cannot be seen. You suffer, and freedom suffers, because there is one fewer among us who has faith that the good will prevail. And without an abundance of such faith, freedom is a lost cause.

Edward Thomson, quoted at the beginning, was doubtless referring to the light of day. However, his dramatically phrased thought is precisely as relevant to the "Light" of an enlightened mind. Phrase it this way:

Light! *Mankind's* resplendent robe; without its flowing inspiration, man is wrapt in gloom.

Seek the Light! Be not distracted from so doing; let nothing stand in the way, not even all the faults of socialists. Henry Ward Beecher offered good counsel: "Every man should keep a fair-sized cemetery in which to bury the faults of his friends." And, I would add, *the faults of his opponents.* If their nonsense causes our gloom, they've won— and without knowing why.

What is my formula for escaping the gloom? I try not to hear or read any of the nonsense—just ignore it. So how do I know what's happening? As to the bad, it's in the atmosphere and can be felt in one's bones, as the saying goes. No careful attention is necessary.

Actually, if I can avoid being distracted by the bad, I can know far more of what's going on than can those who spend their time wandering in this murky swamp; I can spend all of my time on seeking the good—which is enormous. This allows me to draw comparisons between the bad and the good, whereas those who see only the bad can make no comparisons; they are in a blind alley. They are *un*happy, while I am enjoying every moment.

Why seek the light? This is precisely the same as asking, "Why do what's right?" It is only as the right is found and practiced that errors are discovered and dismissed. In our workaday world, it is only as the miraculous wisdom of the free and unfettered market is apprehended that socialism will fall by the wayside.

Wrote Henry Clay, "I would rather be right than be President." So, let us stand with him for the right—for human liberty, peace on earth, good will toward men.

20
EXPLORE AND EXPLORE AND EXPLORE!

Be not chided nor flattered out of your position of perpetual inquiry. Neither dogmatize nor accept another's dogmatism.

—EMERSON

The pursuit of truth demands constant explorations into the unknown. The firm statement by the Sage of Concord appears to provide a solid foundation for my title. The aim in this essay is to diagnose and spell out these thoughts in order better to partake of advice that appears to be unusually wise.

We are surrounded by mystery, and to dramatize the unknown, here is a true story. During the late fifties I was a contestant in the season's most important golf match at my club, St. Andrews. I was in the sandtrap on the 16th and, unless down in two, no chance to win. The trap shot was on the green some 20 feet from the pin—and all uphill. My putt came to a *dead stop* 5 inches from the cup. And then, as if an unseen hand were on my side, it rolled *uphill* and into the cup! An optical illusion? That would have been my conclusion had not the two caddies and my three competitors exclaimed in unison, "That ball had stopped!"

Later on I told a friend of this miracle, and he exclaimed, in disbelief, "That defies the law of gravitation." I replied, "There are laws at work in this universe that neither you nor anyone else ever heard about."

I have had several experiences just as miraculous as this one, and I know of a few other people who have been startled by events equally mysterious. One may assume that millions of individuals, since the dawn of human consciousness, have also experienced the unbelievable. Further, it is more than likely that no two of these phenomena have been identical. And in the folklore of all races credit has been given to medicine men, witch doctors, angels, and all sorts of miracle workers. The leprechauns are a case in point. The ancients of Ireland believed that these elves conferred all the fabulous treasures and miracles that have graced many individuals during the history of man.

To me, the above emphasizes another of Emerson's thoughts: "We lie in the lap of *immense intelligence*"—the Infinite Unknown. We are rocked in the cradles of Creation. Bluntly, relative to the Infinite Unknown, we are no more than "babes in the woods"—no exceptions!

As Cervantes wrote: "The road is always better than the inn." Unfortunately, most people settle on fame or fortune or power as the "inn," and having arrived at these inglorious ends call it quits. They miss the whole point of earthly existence. Realistically, there is no inn, no ultimate point of arrival. It is the road, now and forever—each of us a babe in Creation's cradle probing Infinity, finding one's way. All that matters are the lessons learned along the way.

If the above thoughts be valid, then it is obvious that the spirit of inquiry is the road we mortals should travel, this road stretching endlessly onward and upward. Revelation will be the reward: all the truth one may come by and such virtues as charity, intelligence, justice, reverence, humility, love, and integrity will brighten the ascent.

Why do so many put up at the inn utterly unaware of the road? It is obvious that no one knows all the answers, which is why Emerson's "be not chided nor flattered out of your position of perpetual inquiry" is such excellent counsel. To chide and to flatter are contrasting ways of treating others, and they both have a deadening effect.

Chide: "To speak reprovingly to; to find fault with; blame; rebuke; scold."

A person who is constantly chided or nagged—unless he has the power to disregard it—is given a life sentence. He is reduced to the status of a *Dummkopf* or a nincompoop. He loses sight of the road stretching endlessly onward and upward. For him it's the inn—period! Poor soul!

Flatter: "To praise too much, untruly or insincerely; gratify the vanity of."

Unless one has the wit to disregard such false assessments, flattery, no less than chiding, is another life sentence—growth in awareness, perception, consciousness at an end. Babes in the woods regarding themselves as great men! They are bedded down in that dismal inn which has no windows overlooking the road which leads endlessly onward and upward.

Living by Emerson's "Neither dogmatize nor accept another's dogmatism" is assuredly the way to avoid the afflictions of both chiding and flattery. Dogmatism is defined as a "statement of a belief as if it were an established fact; positiveness when unwarranted or arrogant."

Dogmatizing is one of mankind's major curses. Those who so behave fall into the category of know-it-alls—arrogant, indeed! There is no spirit of inquiry among these millions—in or out of office—who "know" that whatever they believe is "established fact." What they see is all there is! Mysteries? There are none!

Having experienced several mysteries myself, and aware that there are millions times millions unknown to me, the dogmatic pose is an absurdity. The result?

1. No dogmatism directed at others.
2. All dogmatizing by others disregarded.
3. The belief that everyone should be privileged to act creatively as he or she pleases.
4. The spirit of inquiry a leading mission in life.

Finally, how best may one be inspired to pursue the spirit of inquiry? The "second coming" idea is what most appeals to me. Jesus of Nazareth has been presented to mankind as the Perfect Exemplar. And it is predicted that his return will some day grace humanity—the second coming!

Admittedly, my view of this is unorthodox, held by only a few. Here it is: The "second coming" is to be manifested among us mortals. Briefly, we are to strive as best we can and approach as nearly as possible—infinitesimal though it be—His Heavenly Exemplarity. Even supposing this to be an incorrect conclusion, is it not a mortal goal of the first order? Could any ambition better inspire the spirit of inquiry?

Let us, also, bring the second-coming aspiration to the human level. How? By seeking out those few individuals, past and present, who are steps ahead of ordinary mortals—oversouls, if you please— and strive to emulate their excellence. Perpetual inquiry, to repeat Emerson's goal, will be the reward. As examples, two others add their widsom to his:

It is error only, and not truth, that shrinks from inquiry.
—*Thomas Paine*

It is a shameful thing to be weary of inquiry when what we search for is excellence.   —*Cicero*

Thanks to all you oversouls who light our way to the road stretching onward and upward! Explore and explore and explore!

21
REFLECTIONS OF PRAISE AND CRITICISM

In Heav'n's disposing pow'r events
unite,
Nor aught can happen wrong to
him who acts aright.

—HENRY BROOKE

The appropriate method for advancing the freedom way of life is, unquestionably, to live and explain the right way—emphasize the positive—rather than to denounce the countless ways of being wrong. However, there is an important subordinate aspect to explanation and denunciation. It has to do with praise and criticism, a matter worthy of some reflection.

Those who *praise* everything, whether the matter be good or bad, as well as those who *criticize* everybody and everything, act without discrimination. They would not qualify for Brooke's blessing: "Nor aught can happen wrong to him who acts aright."

Praise and criticism may be constructive or destructive, not only to the perpetrator but also to those toward whom the words are directed. Harm may be done to one or both parties, or—on the other hand—genuine good. The following is an attempt to sort the chaff from the wheat, the ignoble from the noble.

Individuals addicted to praising indiscriminately may realize an ignoble ambition. They may gain some favors from politicians and others they praise. At the very least they may be praised in return— an intoxicant that inflates their egos—flattery! The fumes of it invade the brain and make them selfish, proud, and vain!

And what about those who are the objects of undeserved praise? Unless fortified with a rare discrimination, they will believe the folderol. They will overrate themselves. *What a great man am I!* Or, as has been said, "It takes a great deal of grace to be able to bear praise." The gracious way to accept praise is to welcome it as a refreshing breeze passing by—gone with the wind! Admittedly difficult, but it is to act aright!

Does this mean that we should avoid all praise? Of course not! Praise has an important role to play. It should pertain, not to persons, but rather to economic, intellectual, moral, and spiritual achievements. Examples:

- Praise the freedom way of life and all contributions to its better understanding.
- Praise all good thoughts, spoken or written.
- Praise is a debt we owe to virtue.
- Pay tribute to our great mentors of the past by praising their noble works.

"Nor aught can happen wrong to him who acts aright" relates no less to criticism than to praise—perhaps more so. Criticism, for the most part, is of the "thou fool" variety. It is vicious and inflicts its depravity on the perpetrators as much as on those at whom it is aimed.

From the Sermon on the Mount, we read, ". . . whosoever shall say, thou fool, shall be in danger of hell fire," which I take to mean destruction of the self as contrasted with intellectual and spiritual unfoldment or growth in consciousness.

It is absurd to regard others as fools who do not think as I do, believe what I believe, act in my way. For if such were the case—all like me—all would perish. Who is harmed most by this mannerism, others—the "fools"—or I—the fooled? The ignoble I!

I have intimate acquaintances—quite a few of them—who receive more invitations to lecture on the freedom philosophy than they can possibly accommodate. Ever so many in this and other lands seek their counsel. And they know that only those who are seeking can learn. Yet, many of these freedom mentors desert the correct method. Why? They become so exasperated with what's going on that they forsake their reason and yield to their emotions. They call their opponents fools or demagogues or some other derogatory name—criticism at its worst.

Criticism of the "thou fool" variety does far more than offend those at whom it is directed. It causes them to dislike or hate not only the name-callers but the freedom philosophy as well. It hardens them in their socialistic ways and toughens rather than weakens their stand—overcoming made far more difficult.

Now reflect on the name-callers and what this kind of criticism does to them. Not only must we not call them "fools" but, equally as important, we should not even think of them as such. This comes close to being an unattainable discipline but it is one for which we should strive. What happens to us when we think of others in this manner? It results in an overassessment of self: We have all the answers, they have none.

While I believe that collectivist answers are utterly false and that ours are in the direction of truth, I am unaware of anyone who has more than scratched the surface when it comes to understanding and making the case in clarity for the freedom way of life. This being the case, a profound humility should feature our lives—an acknowledgment that we know next to nothing!

It is ever so much easier to preach than to practice what is right. Over the years, I have come to see the error of name-calling, but I still find myself thinking unpleasantly of those whose politico-economic viewpoint is the opposite of mine. It is a habit difficult to overcome.

Is this to suggest that we devotees of freedom should cease all criticizing? Of course not! Criticism, used aright, should never be directed *at persons*; criticize the fallacies of socialism by showing the virtues of freedom. Strict adherence to this tactic has an all-too-seldom discovered blessing not only to self but to the freedom philosophy, freedom of speech being an integral part thereof. Impersonal but proper! This lesson was taught to me 45 years ago.

Back in the early days of the New Deal—the NIRA—the Blue Eagle, so-called—was invoked, a set of strangling controls endorsed by the U.S. Chamber of Commerce, the NAM and most business leaders. On the staff of the Chamber at that time, I learned that one distinguished business leader—unknown to me personally—was severely criticizing this socialistic monstrosity we were sponsoring. "Thinking" that we were right, I called to set him straight. Following my nonsense, he employed a tactic which he rarely used. A very severe critic of all socialistic programs then on the rampage, he emphasized the positive, explaining the freedom philosophy in terms as clear as I have ever heard. That hour's explanation was the birth of my turnabout.

What is criticism's most useful purpose? According to Samuel Johnson, "Criticism, as it was first instituted by Aristotle, was meant as a standard of judging well."

Were we to follow Aristotle's counsel, we would, first and foremost, look critically at our own thoughts, ideas, impulses. Is our understanding of the private ownership, free market, limited government way of life grounded in basic principles or is it merely superficial or imitative?

In the advancement of understanding, are our methods attractive or distractive? Have both praise and criticism been relegated to their appropriate roles?

And, finally, has that all-too-common practice of "reaching others" been replaced by the attempt to get so proficient that others will reach for the freedom-oriented self?

If the answers to these questions are not affirmative, then there is homework to be done. Whether others do it or not is none of my business. What is my business? *My* homework! Interestingly, the more I do the more I find there is to do! And what might have begun as drudgery becomes increasingly joyous.

22

IS THERE
TIME ENOUGH?

*There is nothing covered that shall not be
revealed; and hid that shall not be known.*

—Matthew 10:26

In a spirit of eternal vigilance, let's consider the important matter of advancing an understanding and practice of freedom.

As Aristotle observed, "One may go wrong in many different ways, but right only in one." This applies as pertinently to the subject here at issue as to any other attainment.

First, what are the wrong ways? They are too numerous to list; so to avoid misunderstanding, or pages of explanation, or offense to many of those devoted to freedom, here is the one right way—as I see it: *self-improvement!* This means not only advancing one's own understanding of the freedom philosophy, but achieving an ever-improving clarity in explanation. This is the right way. All the others are wrong and, in my judgment, do more harm than good.

Why is self-improvement the right way? Truth, as related to freedom or to any other subject, cannot be cannonballed into the masses or into any single person. All good and elevating ideas, be they yours or mine or anyone else's, must be sought to be received. Real intellectual gains are made only in response to the law of attraction. In no instance can they be thrust into the mentality of another. All thrusting attempts are distractive rather than attractive and only magnify our problem. They cause the socialistic nonsense to gain by leaps and bounds!

During FEE's 31 years we have heard over and over again words to this effect:

> I agree that self-improvement is highly desirable, but we are facing disaster and your remedy is far too slow. Time is running out. We must get our ideas into the heads of these ignoramuses— and quick!

Most, if not all, of the wrong ways for replacing a growing socialism with a longed-for freedom stem from the notion that there is not time enough for the right way.

Really, the appropriate question is not, "Is there time enough?" but, rather, "Am I enough of an exemplar?" Time is infinite, but I am finite. Thus, when it comes to improving the practice of freedom, my part is to improve myself in my time. Beyond that, there is nothing I can do about it.

If we review the history and timing of good movements, we find that Christianity did not exert its elevating influence on Western Civilization prior to Christ's crucifixion—and not, indeed, for many years thereafter. His exemplarity bore its wonderful fruit long after that shameful event.

Suppose He had held the idea that there wasn't time enough for purity of thought and simple righteousness to result in the conversion of great numbers and had resorted to the wholesale reformation of others during His earthly moments. There would have been no Perfect Exemplar and no Christianity today or ever!

In the realm of mortals also may be found exemplars of the kind that you and I should try our best to emulate—Frederic Bastiat, for instance. Did his wisdom cause a turnabout in his native France during his lifetime (1801–1850)? If anything, the practice of freedom slumped during that period.

Bastiat, however, counseled two Englishmen—Richard Cobden and John Bright—who, in turn, were largely responsible for the advance of the Industrial Revolution as governmental protectionism gave way to free trade—an unprecedented increase of goods and services to the masses. And this, also: at least a million Americans

have read one or more of his works during the past 25 years—
a contribution to our restoration of freedom more than a century
after his death. Bastiat did not live to witness the fruits of his
politico-economic enlightenment. Instead, he labored on his own
improvement in his own time and, in the process, left intellectual
guidelines for others to follow.

Assess the works of our Founding Fathers, writers of the Declaration of Independence, the Constitution, and the Bill of Rights. These
few were inner-directed, seeking an improvement in their own thinking and in their time. Few if any of them lived to witness the remarkable fruits of their joint intellectual, moral, and spiritual labors. Had
that been their consuming zeal—had they paused to lament that
"there's not time enough"—there would have been no American miracle. Those early exemplars did not stop all else to reform the vast
majority who do no politico-economic thinking for themselves. Instead, they sought and discovered a social formula that encouraged
and made it possible for the nonthinkers to cooperate to the best
interests of themselves and all concerned.

There are numerous examples comparable to the above. And,
assuredly, there have been ever so many instances of self-improvement
resulting in monumental advances that have never been fully
recognized and recorded. Indeed, it is certain that countless valuable
social and political gains have been fathered by individuals who were
unaware of their contributions. How come? The fruition of their
exemplary behavior and thinking blessed mankind long after their
mortal moment—often decades or even centuries later!

My admonition (to myself first of all) is that we set not our eyes
upon saving or bettering humanity in our time. If such a result crowns
our efforts, well and good; but our aim should be to strive for truth
and righteousness all the time. To the extent that we succeed in
self-improvement, to that extent will the general human situation
be improved—though no one now knows the precise timing of
the results.

No one knows what will happen in the next minute any more than
he knows what will happen a century from now. It may very well be
that an enlightenment of the past—no one knows how long ago—is
to have its fulfillment right now, that is, in our time. And, by the same
token, anyone's self-improvement of today may achieve fruition in the
far-off future.

Let's have faith that such fulfillment—namely, a restoration of freedom—is in the immediate offing. This faith, however, can be absolutely justified only to the extent that there are individuals who pursue the path of self-improvement. Adherence to what is right—exemplarity—will result in a significant abandonment of the wrong ways, particularly the deadening notion that "There isn't time enough for the right way."

Saint Matthew shares a faith and a promise that should sustain all devotees of freedom: *"There is nothing covered that shall not be revealed; and hid that shall not be known."*

Again, the truth of freedom is about to be revealed and known. For there is not enough darkness in the whole world to put out the light of one small candle. Freedom is light—enlightenment—and cannot be extinguished!

23
WON BY ONE

An individual is as superb as a nation
when he has the qualities that make for a
superb nation.

—WALT WHITMAN

Our earth is but a tiny fraction of the solar system, that is, the sun and all the heavenly bodies that revolve around it. The sun is our star, the sole source of all the light and energy that make earthly life possible. One star, a remarkable **one!** Our galaxy, however, is composed of some 30 billion **ones,** stars that account for the light we occasionally observe in the Milky Way.

Descend now to the earthly level and our own nation. Each individual is but one among more than 200 million. The state of the union—how superb our nation—is determined by the individuals who compose the population. It always has been, is now, and always will be a matter of individuality. If no stars in the citizenry, then nothing splendid is to be expected. But note this: If there be but one who is sufficiently brilliant—a truly remarkable **one**—count on it, ours will be superb nation. Why? *It is light that brings forth the eye!* Thus, how bright the light of a star is the question before us.

During the past 45 years I have become acquainted with thousands of freedom devotees, not only in the U.S.A. but in 22 foreign nations. However, I am unaware of anyone whose quality is superb enough to bring about a superb nation. I know many praiseworthy ones but not the hoped-for remarkable **one.**

My limited vision, however, is not to be taken as proof that there is no **one** amongst us. Who sees all the stars! Reflect on the remarkable **one** of nearly 2,000 years ago. Only a few among the millions on this earth were aware of His existence. Even today, many in the world remain unaware.

To highlight my point, I turn again to an observation by Edmund Burke:

> How often has public calamity been arrested on the very brink of ruin, by the seasonable energy of a single man? Have we no such man amongst us? I am as sure as I am of my being, that one vigorous mind without office, without situation, without public functions of any kind, (at a time when the want of such a thing is felt, as I am sure it is) I say, one such man, confiding in the aid of God, and full of just reliance in his own fortitude, vigor, enterprise, and perseverance, would first draw to him some few like himself, and then that multitudes, hardly thought to be in existence, would appear and troop about him.

Using Burke's observations as guidelines, let's examine today's situation.

What is a public calamity? For geographical pictures have a look at Russia and Red China. Put into words, a public calamity has a double-barreled definition:

> Government ownership and control of the means of production: **The Planned Economy.**
> Government ownership and control of the results of production: **The Welfare State.**

Whether or not this is labeled calamity depends on one's perception. Most Russians and Chinese, born into an authoritarian society, regard their situation not as calamity but as the what-ought-to-be; they do not see beyond their own experiences. And most Americans, born without the gift of seeing through the sham of political babble, are in the same unfortunate fix.

Is the U.S.A. on the brink of ruin? The few who see the glory of the free market, private ownership, limited government way of life—

individual liberty—believe we are heading rapidly toward "the very brink of ruin." The socialistic trend has been gaining momentum each year for the past six or seven decades.

Is there a "seasonable man" amongst us? I am certain, as Burke, that there are numerous persons with this potential, and among us right now. But neither you nor I know who the "seasonable man" is; indeed, that individual himself is unaware. If he so regarded himself, he wouldn't be one. So what is your and my responsibility? It is nothing less than trying to surpass each other—competing for excellence—not necessarily that we'll be the one but that we may be among the few drawn to the "seasonable man."

Is it possible that the "seasonable man" might be an individual who is without office, without situation, without public functions of any kind? Yes, if his mind be adequately vigorous; if righteousness be his first aim in life (confiding in the aid of God), and if he be "full of just reliance in his own fortitude, vigor, enterprise, and perseverance."

All history attests to this truth. Jesus of Nazareth was without office or public functions of any kind, yet he shaped the history of the Western world. And in one degree or another the same might be said of mortals such as Socrates, Maimonides, Francis of Assisi, Thomas Aquinas, Shakespeare, Spinoza, Isaac Newton, Emerson, and Thoreau. In recent times, I need only mention a Ludwig von Mises or an Ezra Taft Benson. And there are many others whose work may have been so much behind the scenes that we know not of them.

Will multitudes, hardly thought to be in existence, appear and troop about him? The millions who today unconsciously follow and troop about present-day socialists will just as unconsciously troop about the **one**. Further, he will be unconscious that he is the **one**, unaware that the exalted ideas and ideals which he exemplifies constitute the driving force.

Finally, what method shall we use in trying to surpass each other in exemplifying freedom ideas and ideals? It is the very opposite of the wrong tactic so often employed: Reaching for others! The right? Striving to achieve that excellence which will cause a few to reach for us! Briefly, it is the improvement of self and not the reforming of others—the power to attract rather than repulse.

Having expressed my views as to what's right and wrong, here are my concluding thoughts as to your role and mine. Merely remember that there is no level to falling or rising stars, to descending or ascending. What then? Strive everlastingly for excellence not only in understanding but for clarity in exposition—clearly as possible without losing the train of thought. Avoid obscurity, labor for simplicity!

Do this and some truly perceptive historian of the future will write of the turnabout now in the offing:

"They Won by One!"

24
•── OUT OF EVIL: GOOD! ──•

Try to find the good in the bad.
The good is always there.
—RUDOLPH STEINER

I choose to be an optimist rather than a pessimist, as related to our present politico-economic decline—and it is not because I am unaware of the decline. My stance is based on a series of exercises begun 20 years ago, Steiner's formula for self-improvement. This requires five minutes of concentration every day for six months—each month a new exercise.[1]

In the fourth month one must contemplate a different bad thing each day until he finds something good in it. Interesting and encouraging, the good is always there! And five minutes is sufficient. One among countless examples: The starling is a messy bird—bad! One day hundreds of them moved across our lawn picking from the soil the grubs of Japanese beetles; their destruction ended—good!

Now to the good that is coming to light as a result of the present decline into socialism. As Horace observed in Rome about 2,000 years ago:

Adversity has the effect of eliciting talents which in times of prosperity would have lain dormant.

•————————

[1] See my *Elements of Libertarian Leadership*, pp. 156–58.

Here is my way of paraphrasing the above as related to this thesis:

Bad notions have the effect of eliciting good ideas which, were all serene and to everyone's satisfaction, would stimulate but little if any mental activity. Dormancy!

Ever since the conclusion of those exercises two decades ago, I have been able to identify countless good and elevating ideas that would have lain dormant had it not been for the bad notions responsible for our decline. While I have featured this discovery—Steiner's, not mine—in all of my lectures on methodology, the inspiration for this essay is a letter just received from an Australian friend.

Somewhat unbelievably, Australia is in a steeper decline than the U.S.A. Wrote my friend, *"One of the good things about our present political mess is an increasing opportunity for me to discuss the ideas of liberty."* Were everything serene and to most people's satisfaction in that country, there would be nothing to evoke his splendid ideas. Were there prosperity, they would have lain dormant!

To put this thesis into focus, to demonstrate how there is always something good in everything bad, imagine a man born at the beginning of life on earth, and still living! By reason of such a life span, his frequency perception would differ from ours. To use a figure of speech, he would see only the forest and not the trees, whereas, we see the trees and not the forest.

Let Walt Disney explain what I mean by frequency perception. He focused his camera on a rose planting, flicking a motion picture film every day or so. When the plant had grown and the rose had bloomed, he put this phenomenon—filmed over many weeks—on the screen so that viewers might witness the development in two or three minutes. That was a dramatic change in frequency perception.

Our imaginary man's frequency perception would be vastly different from ours. About 35 millennia ago, he would have observed a level of humanity known as Cro-Magnon man. From that ancient time until now he would have seen only the emergence of humanity and none of the detail—just the forest and not the trees. Symbolized, it would look something like this:

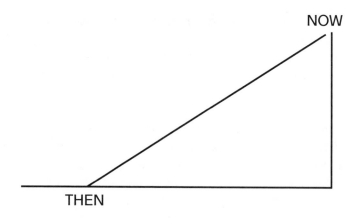

To dramatize the point, put a powerful magnifying glass on this line and have a look at its interior: the detail, the trees in the forest, a look at what a few individuals have seen during the past. The interior would show evolution and devolution in a sequence, evolution inching ahead over the millennia:

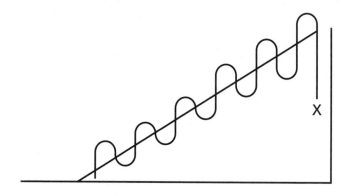

That **X** is to symbolize the present devolutionary position, not only in the U.S.A. but worldwide—no exception! It's the mess we're in—the bad.

This raises the question: How possibly can any good be spawned from our present devolutionary situation? It is so bad—so evil—that many individuals who love liberty do not see or even look for the good. Instead, they indulge in *combative tactics*—name-calling, smearing, and the like. Not an iota of constructive thinking! Or, if not so indulging, they give up the ghost, throw in the sponge. There is no hope; all is lost—so they erroneously conclude.

Parenthetically, combativeness is a belligerent rather than a peaceful tactic. The very essence of freedom is a peaceful way of life and *so must the tactic be*, that is, if we are to be blest by a return to freedom.

A peaceful tactic that works like magic? It is, as Steiner taught, to find the good in the bad. It is always there—a belief for which there are proofs galore.

Here is one among numerous reasons why I know there is always something good in everything bad. The demand for FEE Seminars is increasing beyond our ability to accommodate. During the past year, we have conducted 23 from east to west—Georgia to Hawaii and in between. Aside from the Seminars at FEE, all have been sought by those interested in learning the freedom philosophy, not one promoted by us. What stimulates this yearning for learning? Nothing less than the bad we are experiencing! It is the current socialism that inspires a desire for understanding the freedom way of life, the bad that causes a search for the good—*on the part of a few*.

A few? Devolutionary slumps have quite a record of creating anti-agents—always an infinitesimal minority. But note this: On each occasion, it has been and will continue to be a matter of leadership. In every instance, one or two among the anti-agents will be up topside, "at the head of the class," as we say.

Christianity was led by the Perfect Exemplar. He had a dozen Disciples—anti-agents—spawned by the bad that was rampant at that time in history. The turnabout in England following the Napoleonic Wars—from mercantilism to the Industrial Revolution—was led by Richard Cobden and John Bright. They had a small number of coworkers: anti-agents. The same can be said about the American Miracle. A few of our Founding Fathers led the way to the most miraculous politico-economic turnabout in all history!

Instead of lamenting the present devolutionary position, I applaud it. Why such an unorthodox attitude? Merely have a look at the devolutionary-evolutionary sequence. Each devolutionary slump serves as a springboard—an inspiration—that leads to the next evolutionary attainment. For proof, no more is required than a look at the historical record. Its instruction to us? Evolution, emergence, growth, awareness, perception, consciousness inching ahead as time goes on! Were it not for the stimulus to find the good which the bad evokes, humanity would still be at the Cro-Magnon level!

Back to the Seminars and their participants. Why are they present? It's the bad that's on the rampage! They have become anti-agents, searching for the good by reason of the evil.

A point that should be emphasized: Suppose you were in charge of the Cosmic Design. Would you pap feed the population—"money or favors from political office"—or would you give them obstacles to overcome? Obviously, you would choose the latter, for it is an observed fact that the *act* of overcoming leads to the *art* of becoming! Life has no higher purpose than rising to one's intellectual, moral, and spiritual potential—*becoming!*

Another appropriate suggestion to participants: Please note what's going on above your shoulders that would lie dormant were all serene and satisfying. Your *newborn* activity is a heavenly blessing emanating from our current devolutionary position. So why not join in applauding this socialistic mess for your own sake and for freedom's sake? It has made an anti-agent of you against the know-nothings who would run our lives. Thus are you inspired to help achieve that glorious ideal in which each is able to act creatively as he pleases!

Finally, a thought worth repeating: Our present-day anti-agents are growing in an understanding of freedom and its supporting virtues. It is this kind of growth, and this only, that energizes the magnetism which causes others to seek one's tutorship. Only those who seek enlightenment can become enlightened! Thus, those who see the truly good spawned by the present bad are responsible for more and more anti-agents, all of whom grace mankind and by reason of their love of liberty!

25

HUMILITY: THE REMEDY FOR EGOMANIA?

God dwells not in temples made by human hands; his abiding place is the humble and contrite heart.

—THE HOLY BIBLE

If Infinite Consciousness [God]—Wisdom and Righteousness—does not originate in you or me or any individual, why then do so many of us pretend and behave otherwise, that is, in fits of egomania? It seems worthwhile to reflect on this problem.

Egomania is "abnormally, excessive egotism." And egotism? It "...is constant, excessive reference to oneself in speaking and or writing." Briefly, an egomanic is an individual who regards himself as *a source* of wisdom; whatever he speaks or writes or conceives is original; there is nothing above his finite mind!

Persons afflicted with the notion that they are the originators of wise thoughts and ideas are prone to regard any repetition of them by others as plagiarism. Goethe—one of the great thinkers of modern times—voiced a profound but neglected truth: "All truly wise ideas have been thought already thousands of times." Any person who claims to originate a truly wise idea might just as well regard himself as the source of Creation! Those of us who regard ourselves as *source* are victims of an all-too-common affliction—egomania.

The reason for this may well be that the self-assumed originator had not previously seen the idea in print. Now, no person has ever read more than a tiny fraction of all that has been printed. And, assuredly, most of the truly wise ideas during the past several thousand years may have been neither written nor even voiced. All of us have ideas that might remain silently in the mind, while nevertheless guiding our actions.

Everything—no exception—is mysterious. No one knows why grass is green, for instance, or what electricity is. And of all the mysteries, Infinite Wisdom or Consciousness—how Creation works its wonders—is infinitely beyond finite man's comprehension. A few—past and present—have freed themselves from egomania. How? By becoming aware that Creation is *the* Source, not they themselves.

The few who have been or are aware that they are not *the* Source quite properly ascribe the reception of truly wise ideas to Creation. Numerous are the ways these few describe such heavenly phenomena. To me, Emerson's is among the brilliant acknowledgments:

> We lie in the lap of immense intelligence [Creation], which makes us receivers of its truth and organs of its activities. When we discern justice, when we discern truth, *we do nothing of ourselves, but allow a passage of its beams.*

A passage of its beams suggests that the immense intelligence is an omnipresent radiation. Required of us mortals is to see how much of it we can intercept or tune in—make of ourselves as much of a receiving set as possible.

For evidence that this is a radiation, observe tune-ins occurring to persons unknown to each other—*simultaneously!* One among countless examples: penicillin was discovered by an American medical student and by another in a foreign country—at the same time! This phenomenon is often referred to as "coincidental thinking." A more accurate term would be "coincidental reception." Dr. Carl Jung, the famous Swiss psychiatrist, wrote a book confirming these miracles.[1]

---

[1] *Synchronicity* by Dr. Carl Jung (Princeton University Press, 1973).

What we must keep in mind is the infinite nature of this radiation. We can assume that it contains all there is in the Cosmic Design, now and forever, man having perceived but an infinitesimal fraction of it. Further, one's reception, such as it is, depends on his potentialities and uniqueness. Briefly, one's emergence depends on the few beams he is capable of intercepting.

Is any of us able to assess the enormity of these beams? In my judgment, it would be easier to count the components of the solar system's atmosphere in which we earthlings live and breathe or all the components in the atmospheres of an ever-expanding universe. Why? We possess but finite consciousness. At best, ours are but infinitesimal glimmers of Infinite Consciousness [God]. We should recognize that it is impossible for anyone to *comprehend* Infinite Consciousness or infinite space or infinite time.

However, an *awareness* of infinity is possible. How? There are numerous ways. For my explanation of an easy way, see chapter 10, page 45.

History affords an excellent example of this phenomenon. According to the anthropologists, there existed about 35,000 years ago a level of humanity referred to as Cro-Magnon man. No question about it, there are millions in today's world who have intercepted ever so many more of these heavenly beams than did those beings centuries ago. In this progression we witness man's earthly purpose—growing, emerging, evolving, bit by bit in consciousness. It is only consciousness that is immortalized, our earthly moments being but your and my beginnings.

It seems plain to me that Infinite Consciousness—Wisdom and Righteousness—"dwells not in temples made by human hands." Those who believe that they are sources or originators suffer from egomania.

It also seems evident that "his abiding place is the humble and contrite heart." Only in those who know that they know not can the beams of *immense intelligence* find an abiding place. The ever-seeking eye is to be found among those who are humble. Their eyes are cast toward the Infinite Unknown.

The blessings of humility were recognized long before the Holy Bible was written. Samplings:

Humility is the foundation of all virtues.   *—Confucius*

Whoever humbleth himself shall be exalted.   *—Lao-tse*

Socrates revealed his humility:

That man thinks he knows everything whereas he knows nothing. I know nothing, but I know that I know nothing.

Centuries later, St. Augustine made many contributions to the wisdom of having a humble heart. Here are two:

It was pride that changed angels into devils; it is humility that makes men as angels.

The sufficiency of my merit is to know that my merit is not sufficient.

Wrote St. Bernard:

It is no great thing to be humble when you are brought low; but to be humble when you are praised is a great and rare attainment.

Now to modern times:

True humility
The highest virtue, mother of them all.   *—Tennyson*

Humility, like darkness, reveals the heavenly lights.   *—Thoreau*

No one knows very much.   *—Kettering*

No one knows more than one-millionth of one
per cent of anything.   *—Edison*

The above are but a few well-known testimonials to the "humble and contrite heart." As with all truly wise ideas, "They have already been thought thousands of times"— perhaps millions of times!

Goethe used the terms Nature and God as virtually interchange-able. He referred to Nature as the Divinity. Johann Peter Eckermann, his devoted associate, kept an almost daily record of his visits with Goethe during the last nine years of the great man's life. The result is *Conversations with Goethe*, a book filled with wisdom.[2]   On February 13, 1829, Eckermann wrote in his journal, "Dined with Goethe alone." He then reported the wisdom that flowed from this scholar's mind, including one of my favorite gems:

> Nature understands no jesting; she is always true, always serious, always severe; she is always right, and the errors and faults are always those of man. The man incapable of appreciating her she despises and only to the apt, the pure, and the true, does she resign herself and reveal her secrets.

The errors and faults are always those of man, egomania being among the enfeebling faults. However, when man accords to God, to Nature, to Divinity *the source* of Wisdom and Righteousness, humility rules the soul.

When the great I-Am gives way to I-know-not, the mind opens to Infinite Consciousness. A yearning for learning becomes life's highest goal—"she resigns herself and reveals her secrets."

The freedom to act creatively as anyone pleases is among the secrets revealed. Hail to humility!

---

[2] New York: E. P. Dutton & Company, 1935.

NAME INDEX

Acton, Lord, 48
Aesop, 36
Anderson, Maxwell, 39
Aramburu (General), 7
Aristotle, 43
Arnold, Matthew, 20
Augustine, Saint, 114

Bastiat, Frederic, 13, 99
Beecher, Henry Ward, 88
Bernard, Saint, 114
Bradford, Ralph, 62
Bradford, William, 70
Bright, John, 3, 99, 109
Brillat-Savarin, Anthelme,
    64–65
Brooke, Henry, 94
Bryan, William Jennings, 65
Bryant, William Cullen, 30
Burgess, John W., 54
Burns, Robert, 31
Burke, Edmund, 4, 18, 58,
    103, 104

Campora, Hector, 7
Cecil, Richard, 76
Cervantes, 91
Cicero, 37, 65, 93
Clay, Henry, 66, 89
Cobden, Richard, 3, 99, 109
Confucius, 114
Congreve, William, 34

Day, Holman F., 86
Disney, Walt, 107
Dulles, John Foster, 51
Eckermann, Johann Peter,
    46, 115
Edison, Thomas Alva, 25, 114
Elder, George, 74
Emerson, Ralph Waldo, 5, 12,
    16, 36, 58, 72, 73, 74, 90,
    104, 112

Fisher, M. F. K., 64
Frondizi, Arturo, 7

Goethe, Johann Wolfgang,
    5, 15, 17, 19, 43, 44, 46,
    57, 61, 63, 65, 66, 67,
    111, 115
Gracián, Baltasar, 72

Hall, Verna, 83
Hamilton, Sir William, 32
Hayek, Friedrich von, 50
Heraclitus, 31
Hogshead, Thomas, 9
Horace, 36, 106
Hugo, Victor, 67

Jefferson, Thomas, 71
Jesus, 92, 99, 104
John, 36
Johnson, Samuel, 97
Jung, Carl, 112

Kettering, C. F., 114

La Fontaine, 37
Lamb, Charles, 37
Lao-tse, 114
Lee, David G., 26
Leo XIII, Pope, 53
Leonardo da Vinci, 2
Lincoln, Abraham, 66
Lombardi, Michael, 16
Longfellow, Henry Wadsworth, 31
Lotharius I, 31
Lynch, Alberto Benegas, 7

Marx, Karl, 70, 83
Matsushita, Konosuke, 17
Matthew, 98, 101
Meurier, Gabriel, 11
Mirabeau, 64
Mises, Ludwig von, 77

Nock, Albert Jay, 75

Ogden, Charles, 11
Ovid, 23, 31

Paine, Thomas, 93
Perón, Juan Domingo, 7
Poe, Edgar Allan, 59

Richards, Ivor, 11
Rogge, Benjamin A., 6, 8, 9, 10
Rojas (Admiral), 7

Sarpi, Paolo, 49
Schumpeter, Joseph A., 19, 22, 23
Shakespeare, William, 51, 81, 83, 84, 104
Sheldon, Arthur F., 17
Shenfield, Arthur, 23
Sheridan, Richard, 36
Smith, Adam, 3, 34
Socrates, 25, 29, 34, 35, 36, 37, 51, 58, 73, 82, 84, 104, 114
Sparks, Bertel, 17, 68
Spinoza, 44
Spurgeon, Charles, 37
Steiner, Rudolph, 106
Stevenson, Robert Louis, 32

Tennyson, Alfred, 1–3, 59, 61, 114
Thomson, Edward, 85
Thoreau, Henry David, 104, 114

Washington, George, 4, 24
Weaver, Richard, 11
White, Andrew Dickson, 48–49, 63, 65
Whitman, Walt, 102
Wilmot, John, 86